Praise for
*The Shadow of His Hand*

"Judith Couchman has helped us realize that where there is a shadow, there is always light. Especially when the shadow cast is the shadow of His hand. Losses lead to findings, and pain leads to peace, if we respond rightly to life's troubles. *The Shadow of His Hand* will help the broken to find blessing, the fearful to discover courage, and the one who is about to give up, hope. In the end pain drives us to God and deeper into His unlimited resources—if we allow it."

—JILL BRISCOE, author, speaker,
and minister-at-large for Elmbrook Church in Wisconsin

"With honesty, vulnerability, and a willingness to write out of her own brokenness, Judith Couchman recognizes that life isn't always fair, fun, or easy. This compilation of short essays gives the reader permission to acknowledge personal pain and provides answers that avoid common clichés. If your life isn't perfect, read this book."

—CAROL KENT, president, Speak Up Speaker Services
and author of *Becoming a Woman of Influence*

"There is truth in the old adage that 'misery loves company' because nobody knows what it's like or how it hurts until they've been there. Judith Couchman has been there, and her writing, as well as excerpts from other fine authors who've known the bite of the dark side of life, ministers to others who are hurting. Her words are like a soothing balm to a stinging wound."

—LISA TAWN BERGREN,
best-selling author of *The Bridge*

"I love honest books...and this is one. Judith is my companion of choice for exploring the pain and paradoxes of life's unfulfilled longings. Through compelling stories, soul-baring memoirs, and thoughtful reflection on Scripture, she deftly and compassionately shines a light on our yearnings...and then leads us into the presence of the God who comforts and strengthens us. If you've ever been battered or bruised by life (and who hasn't?), you should read this book."

—SUE KLINE, editor of *Discipleship Journal*
and author of *Your Money and Your Life*

"*The Shadow of His Hand* is a wise, warm, and wonderful book. Thanks, Judith, for sharing on these pages some honest sustenance for our hungry souls. Your openness not only makes the rugged terrain we're traveling through less lonely, but it also helps illuminate for us the journey home."

—DEBRA EVANS, author of *Women of Courage*
and *Soul Satisfaction*

"In *The Shadow of His Hand*, Judith Couchman's own story of finding grace in the midst of loss is joined by words of encouragement from a choir of wise fellow witnesses. In the company of such believers, no reader can feel alone."

—FREDERICA MATHEWES-GREEN,
columnist and author of *The Illumined Heart*

# *The*
# SHADOW *of*
# HIS HAND

*When Life Disappoints,*

*You Can Rest in*

*God's Comfort and Grace*

## JUDITH COUCHMAN

WATERBROOK
PRESS

THE SHADOW OF HIS HAND
PUBLISHED BY WATERBROOK PRESS
2375 Telstar Drive, Suite 160
Colorado Springs, Colorado 80920
*A division of Random House, Inc.*

ISBN 1-57856-092-6

Published in association with the literary agency of Alive Communications, Inc., 7680 Goddard Street, Suite 200, Colorado Springs, CO 80920.

Printed in the United States of America
2002—First Edition

10 9 8 7 6 5 4 3 2

*For the Vision writers.*

---

I have put my words in your mouth
and covered you with the shadow of my hand.

—ISAIAH 51:16

# Contents

# Acknowledgments

Usually in the acknowledgments I thank people who assisted me during the process of writing a manuscript. But this time I'm expressing gratitude to those who've helped me live the principles in this book. Those concepts had to be thoroughly experienced before my hands touched a keyboard to type. However, I didn't set out to write a book about pain and difficulty, nor did my family and friends anticipate it. They just lovingly cheered me on, and what I learned eventually spilled onto these pages.

To Nancy Lemons, my eternal friend, I owe so much. She senses when I need comfort or just a good talk and calls me from Chicago at uncannily opportune times. Thanks for listening to my rambling, believing in me as a career writer, and loving me thoroughly despite all the flaws and mistakes. You are unshockable and irreplaceable, both practically and philosophically supportive, and I treasure you.

Similar support characterizes Melissa Munro, my remarkable niece. Though twenty years younger, she possesses wisdom that I need and lets me hand my real self to her, without losing her love and respect for me. She also typed the excerpts in this book, with no charge except wasting time together. Along with my love, I'll always offer that gladly, with or without a project in hand. Melissa learned loving ways from her mother and my older sister, Shirley Honeywell, who talked to God about me more than I'll ever know. Thank you, Shirley, for your continued prayers.

When I could no longer afford my home, Mary Brosa cheerfully took in me and "the boys," though her invitation increased the pet population in her house to four goofy, brawling cats. Monet, Wolfie, and I thank you for sharing your home, food, humor, and heart with us.

A group of praying women, spread across the country, played a vital role in keeping my needs and requests before God. I credit them for the breakthroughs and other everyday miracles in my life. Some are "official" prayer team members, while others interceded for specific events or situations. They included Joan Badzik, Charette Barta, Helen Benson, Betty Bradley, Mary Brosa, Mary Bundy, Jan Condon, Opal Couchman, Win Couchman, Merry Dankanich, Kathy Fisher, Jan Frank, Madalene Harris, Karen Hilt, Tammy Holliday, Shirley Honeywell, Karen Howells, Keri Kent, Linda Kraft, Susan Lee, Nancy Lemons, Beth Lueders, Lisa Marzano, Marian McFadden, Cindy Miller, Melissa Munro, Victoria Munro, Kay O'Connor, Arlene Ord, Rita Rocker, Anne Scott, Kathie Schroeder, Naomi Trujillo Smith, Connie Swanson, Mary Jane Tynan, Lucibel VanAtta, Midge Wietzema, and Kathe Wunnenberg. There are probably others I don't know about, or forgot to list, so please forgive me if you're not mentioned. This doesn't mean I appreciate your prayers any less, just that my brain exceeds forty years old.

Others, both friends and strangers, prayed, prophesied, or helped deliver me from spiritual attack. Thanks to the compassionate Andy Landis, the hilarious duo of Joan Badzik and Juanda Green, my insightful pastor Dutch Sheets, and the powerful group of Bobbie Byerly, Ceci Sheets, Quin Sherer, and another woman whose name I don't even know. In addition, the original Vision Group unwittingly ministered to me each year at our retreat, affirming and encouraging my calling, plus laughing and loving me through those amazing weekends. Thanks to the women who've passed through or still belong to that writers' group.

Still others provided rest and joy. I'm grateful to Beth Kawasaki and Susan Smith who loaned me their beach houses for uninterrupted writing and to Laurel Justice who took me to her family's house in the mountains. Laurel also prodded me with ideas and discussions that kept my artist soul awake, and she has grown into a precious friend. Chris and Nancy Lemons also offered me their family's cabin in the woods, where I wrote in blessed winter solitude.

On the pragmatic side, I also thank those who offered gifts and loans to fill in the financial gaps but wish to remain anonymous. Plus Janel Ferguson, who repeatedly listened to the many up-and-down details about the writing life.

At WaterBrook I thank Dan Rich, Rebecca Price, and Erin Healy for not giving up on me when chronic physical pain and other intrusions delayed writing this book. Also, kudos to Erin for her kind and insightful editing, to Laura Wright for guiding me through production, and to John Hamilton for his thoughtful design.

Most important, I thank my mother Opal Couchman once again for loving and believing in me as a person and a writer—and for supporting, reprimanding, and encouraging me through difficult days. She's a gentle hope behind all that I do.

# The Wounded Healer's Hand

Looking back at my days so far, I've never pulled life all together. Not for a moment or even a nanosecond. But God knows I've tried. Somewhere I gathered the notion that if I worked diligently, heaping accomplishments in my to-do basket, I'd someday stunningly emerge as a Woman to Admire, brimmed with bounty and graciousness. I'm still scavenging for the iota of spiritual truth in that supposition, but I doubt I'll ever pluck it from life's wildness or my weedy heart. Reality proved that the more I heaped, the more I crumbled, and the more I crumbled, the more I exposed my wounds, desperation, and disappointment. Finally, exhausted and facedown and stuck in the brier, I reached up for a hand.

Surprisingly, the hand didn't haul me under sunbeams to pick off the nettles, brush away the soil, and nudge me back on the pebbly path. Instead, it joggled me deep into the shadows of obscurity, far from the maddening brambles, to lie begrudgingly in the coolness and finally feel the pain of my pricked and sunstroked soul. I hated it. Friends seemed to bask in the sunshine, traipsing to lovely destinations, oblivious to my damage. So why were my aspirations truncated? Why this peculiar, singled-out attention? Yet with time—a time that lingered and lounged, though I urged it to pass by briskly—I identified the darkness as a privileged place. In the dimness I recognized the masterful Wounded Healer. His tender hand had installed me there. He more than anyone understands the longings of a broken heart. Though my wounds throbbed, I resided under his watchful care. I could rest.

■   ■   ■

When life disappoints—when it batters and bruises us; when we batter and bruise ourselves—God places us in the shadow of his hand to quiet, succor, and strengthen us. Though we struggle against the solitary darkness, we need its comfort and protection to recover and relearn how to live. The shadow is our refuge and fortress, though circumstances and personal failings rage about and within us. The Almighty weathers difficulties along with his children, sheltering them with himself (Psalm 91:1-2).

In the shadow, God also uses the hardship to change us for the better, if we'll withstand the initial agony of his lancing our festered hearts to begin the transformation process. The difficulty that bares our wounds can range from a trifling nuisance to a full-scale, life-ending trauma. Over the last six years, God has unveiled my sheerly disguised need for change and healing through job loss, personal sin, family fissures and illnesses, career failure, financial deprivation, chronic physical pain, relationship blunders, intense spiritual warfare, and the loss of my home. I've withstood public criticism and misunderstanding, feared bankruptcy, been rejected by friends, and struggled against my propensity toward denial, disobedience, and procrastination. At times I've wanted God to "just take me up there" because I keep messing up down here. Instead, he's insisted that my responsibility on earth isn't "being good," but rather, accepting and reflecting his grace.

Still, some of you opening this book have endured far more hardship than I ever will. Your stories speak of searing pain, unending disappointment, and justifiable questioning vastly greater than mine. You're also better acquainted with the profundity and necessity of dwelling in the shadow of God's hand. Because of this, I've struggled and stalled writing these pages, feeling inadequate and baffled by the task. Who am I to write about the perplexing problem of pain, when the suffering but sinless Job couldn't comprehend it? But again, God requests that I be myself—a memoirist, not a theologian or a psychologist—and that I write about what I'm learning with the hope of casting insight and encouragement on your struggles, inviting you to nestle under the shadow too.

With this mandate, I've written about my uneven and ongoing journey, wanting to keep you plodding toward personal transformation and a meaningful walk with God, despite the troubles in your life. That type of perseverance isn't simple, but given time and surrender, it can be personally and spiritually rewarding. I've also placed my stories within the context of several stages we pass through while encountering, learning from, and changing through difficulty. From the first shock waves of loss through the dulling dailyness of pain or discontent, learning to thrive and not just survive is a long-term process. Through it all, God guides us bit by bit and hand in hand toward a new understanding of him and his purposes.

But one author can't experience or know it all, so to broaden and deepen the perspective, I've interspersed classic and contemporary writings of Christians who've faced life's complexities and found God shining into the darkness. Even if you discard my words and only read their essays, I feel certain of the Lord's comfort extended to you. So whatever you select from these pages, read with the assurance that God loves you intensely, wants to heal your wounds, and beckons you to safety in the shadow of his hand.

—Judith Couchman

# Psalm 91

He who dwells in the shelter of the Most High
will rest in the shadow of the Almighty.
I will say of the LORD, "He is my refuge and my fortress,
my God, in whom I trust."

Surely he will save you from the fowler's snare
and from the deadly pestilence.
He will cover you with his feathers,
and under his wings you will find refuge;
his faithfulness will be your shield and rampart.
You will not fear the terror of night,
nor the arrow that flies by day,
nor the pestilence that stalks in the darkness,
nor the plague that destroys at midday.
A thousand may fall at your side,
ten thousand at your right hand,
but it will not come near you.
You will only observe with your eyes
and see the punishment of the wicked.

If you make the Most High your dwelling
—even the LORD, who is my refuge—
then no harm will befall you,
no disaster will come near your tent.
For he will command his angels concerning you
to guard you in all your ways;
they will lift you up in their hands,
so that you will not strike your foot against a stone.
You will tread upon the lion and the cobra;
you will trample the great lion and the serpent.

"Because he loves me," says the LORD, "I will rescue him;
I will protect him, for he acknowledges my name.
He will call upon me, and I will answer him;
I will be with him in trouble,
I will deliver him and honor him.
With long life will I satisfy him
and show him my salvation."

# PART ONE

# When Life Interrupts

We all harbor images of an ideal and obtainable lifestyle. But eventually something intrudes and a painful gap yawns between our desires and reality. We experience losses of all kinds and the disappointment sinks deep.

As Christians we're not immune from the feelings and misunderstandings that emerge when life interrupts. We live in a fallen world, and though we search for a time when "everything works out," reality insists that life is flawed and fragile. So are we. Yet if we belong to God, we also possess a dependable hope.

# An Unexpected Truth

*Unless you expect the unexpected,*
*you will never find [truth],*
*For it is hard to discover and hard to attain.*

—HERACLITUS

I sat at the desk with my palms propping up my forehead so it wouldn't lunge forward and bang on the unforgiving metal. That would call an ever-loyal assistant to my side of the office divider, and I didn't want to explain that she worked for a burnout, though I suspect she already knew it and politely obliged me. I felt beyond tired. Trying to focus on the financial report inches from my face, I imagined my eyeballs falling out, cartoonlike, attached by an invisible string and resting on the printout, perhaps to help me focus.

*How much have we spent on telephone expenses?* I squinted at the figures again, imploring my eyeballs to wake up. Well, at least my ears still worked. They alerted me to a rustling in the room, and I jerked up my head, with eyeballs snapping back and focusing just in time. It was our magazine's publisher, followed by the financial manager. For the chief editor of a publication, that's seldom a reassuring duo to have invade your office. The publisher might be a welcome sight, but not those two together. That combo almost always sniffs of messy business.

And it did. Long story short, after only four issues we could no longer afford to publish the magazine. Unless we raised a million dollars in the next thirty days, it wouldn't survive. Neither would I, nor our carefully acquired editorial staff. We'd all lose our jobs. Part of me expected this pronouncement; the other part didn't. (In most companies even the most guarded information somehow leaks and rumors spread.) At this point I knew a million dollars in a month formed an impossible goal, but I still couldn't believe we'd crash. Not after all our incessant work and prayer. God wouldn't allow that, would he?

Years later I can talk about this incident matter-of-factly. But back then, after the bad-news boys left my office, I locked myself in an empty conference room and shook with silent sobs, too numb and exhausted to create noise. I couldn't decide whether to muster up faith or begin packing. For a decade I'd dreamed and prayed about launching a spiritually attuned magazine for women, especially those who lingered at the edges of Christianity and needed inner replenishment. For another four years I planned, raised money, and shaped the publication, mostly while holding down a full-time job elsewhere in the sponsoring organization. It'd hoard too many pages to describe how God directed each step; how I learned that he, not I, owned this project. He'd spun miracles and assembled a small group of creatives to ensure the magazine's launch. (Even today nobody can dissuade me of God's involvement.) It looked like a long-awaited dream come true.

On the other hand, I worked so much I fell to depression and fatigue. The pressure of a startup surfaced the worst in some staff members, and I felt chronically frustrated, stuck in a "don't manage it this way" example from a How to Work with Difficult People seminar. Critics within and outside the organization misunderstood the magazine's mission, and some accused me of apostasy. I tried to please everybody and satisfied hardly anybody under the constant threat of unrealistic deadlines and a shutdown because of insufficient funds. I canceled my personal life, quit my passion called writing, thickened my skin toward criticism, lagged behind because of insufficient help, struggled with chronic back pain aggravated by stress, and weathered it all because I believed God would reward us in the end. We'd own a magazine that met women's deep needs, and of course, he'd bless me for my perseverance. I would be living proof that a good God fulfills our heart's desires.

Instead, the new fiscal year found me alone and draped on the living room couch, unemployed and afraid of losing my home, stunned by the biggest flop of my life. When I tired of the pain, I curled up and slept for hours. But even my dreams seemed to ask, "God, what have you done? How will you disappoint me next?"

It's probably best I didn't hear anything back. I'd have been horrified by the answer. "Well, Judy, now I'm going to take you through the worst of times and the best of times. Circumstances may grow worse, but I'm going to change you for the better." My brain would have frozen on the first half of that so-called reassurance. Things might get worse? Who in their right earthly mind wants to hear that? It took a few years for me to realize that only God can adjust our spiritual senses to discover the blessings in brokenness. Only he can teach this truth in a comprehensible lesson and free us with it.

An anonymous contemplative from the fourteenth century claimed we exist in a "cloud of unknowing" that separates us from God. It's a darkness that obscures our understanding of the Maker and his ways.[1] I think that's where most of us stand when the unexpected hits, especially if we're accosted by a dastardly something or someone we'd rather not meet. Suddenly we don't understand much of anything because God didn't perform as we thought he would or should. We're hurt and afraid, confused and probably angry. Who knows what our wobbly selves might threaten to do? *If Somebody up there still cares, he'd better reach through that cloud and clutch us with all his might.*

And that's what God says he'll do.

---

*Then you will know the truth,*
*and the truth will set you free.*

—JOHN 8:32

# Where's the Script?

*If this were played upon a stage now,*
*I could condemn it as an improbable fiction.*

—WILLIAM SHAKESPEARE,
*TWELFTH NIGHT*

In high school my greatest desire centered on winning the lead in our school musical. Other girls languished about boyfriends, cheerleading, popularity, or reigning as homecoming queen, but I wanted to act and sing my way to Central High fame. Never mind that most students and teachers considered me shy and awkward and I probably didn't possess enough talent to pull it off fabulously. It still remained my dream, and sometimes dreams debunk realism.

However, a few people thought I might win the lead role during my senior year. The previous fall as a junior I'd captured a small starring spot in the musical; seniors played the rest of the leading parts. Often a junior with this distinction moved up to a major role as a senior. Besides some decent grades, it's what I wanted most from high school.

Imagine my disappointment, then, when I didn't win the lead and the choir director awarded it to my friend. He didn't even name me as understudy (he awarded that to another friend), and instead, my misguided teacher added me to the list of dancers. I hadn't auditioned for a dancing part, had never hoofed in my life, and possessed the physical grace of a heifer. Too hurt to face my teacher and explain that dancing horrified me, I struggled through the routines that required tons more coordination than acting/singing roles. Even though I'm short, the choreographer tucked me in the back row of dancers, extreme stage right. (Perhaps if I collapsed, I could conveniently crawl offstage?) My stumbling around embarrassed me and disturbed people at my church who declared dancing "unchristian" and designed by the devil. Still, I endured the rehearsals.

I also assumed the duties of stage manager, and a few weeks into rehearsals, the music teacher drove me home after a late practice. I don't know what possessed him, but as we pulled up to my house he cleared his throat and dropped an emotional bomb. "You know, Judy, I should have given you the lead role. I'm sorry that I didn't. At the time I was concerned that your singing voice wouldn't project loud enough."

Loud enough? If he wanted to hear loud, he could listen to the sound of my shattering heart. (I couldn't dance, but I still had a firm flair for the dramatic.) Somehow I managed more rehearsals and three performances, and I kept the photos to prove it.

■   ■   ■

That disappointing episode must have imbedded deep in my psyche because three decades later I still dream about tryouts, rehearsals, and stage faux pas. These performance dreams emerge when I'm stressed, and lately that's most of the time. I've dreamt so many unsettling variations, I recently started recording them in a hand-sized journal lying on a nightstand inches from my bed, with the hope of understanding why they still plague me. When I wake up I can roll over and scribble, attempting not to lose the details to morning rituals. It's almost like jotting notes for a novel; the story line keeps building toward a suspenseful conclusion.

The dreams initially centered on the choir director sponsoring tryouts for a musical, but he won't let me audition. I beg, insisting I'll do better this time, but he won't budge. Sometimes I'm my current age, explaining that as an adult I'm more confident and can perform much better than "those kids." Next the dreams shifted to attending the tryouts, but I'm unprepared and can't remember the lyrics to a song or focus on the fuzzy-lined script. I'm panicked, certain I'm about to fail, humiliating myself before everyone present, which seems like the entire world.

These days the slumbering stories finally land me on stage with a role in the performance. Unfortunately, dread and dismay join me. I can't recall rehearsing, can't figure out my cues, can't keep pace with the other actors. Often my frustration focuses on the libretto: everyone flips through one but me. Frustrated, I cry, "Where's the script? Would somebody please give me a script?" Nobody responds, or if I finally hold one in my trembling hands, I can't find the pages with my character's lines. Or once again the words blur and I can't read them. Once again I wind up missing what's important to me.

A friend told me that when we recognize a dream's message, it'll disappear from our subconscious, so after years of dreaming about the stage, I've decided to decipher its meaning. I've culled several promising interpretations from these metaphorical stories, and I'm sorting out their causes and remedies. (So please don't send me your ideas.) I've thought about my "Where's the script?" question, privately using it as a humorous response when I feel clueless. Much like the "Where's the beef?" ad that tickled the nation years back, it's grown into an overused slogan, but for an audience of one.

I suspect, though, that lots of us would like to ask the script question, especially when life swerves in an unexpected direction. "Where's the script? Would somebody please tell me what to do now? I'm flailing over here." It seems we're the only one out of sync, unable to flow with the performance. Nobody told us about panic and missteps, and there's no prompter in the orchestra pit feeding lines to us. Life didn't hand us a libretto. Even worse, when we listen for God, pain and confusion freeze the senses, blocking him out, and if we strain for the Voice, we only hear the buzzing in our brains.

What can we do? Actually, at first we needn't do much. It takes time to thaw the numbness, soak in the reality, grapple with the pain. This process prevents us from cowering in denial, creating greater calamity for ourselves later, living with frozen emotions and waking up from nightmares for the next thirty years. When my father died I heard it's best for a widow not to make major decisions and changes for at least a year. My mother would agree with that now, regretting a few things she sloughed off too soon. After the magazine's demise an older friend advised, "Don't try to do anything now. Just rest. God will speak when it's time."

Even the teacher who sentenced me to performance nightmares dispensed wise advice to choir members after he announced the leads for our musical. "If you didn't get a part, give yourself time to feel bad." He believed that when we're hurt we should allow ourselves enough time to grieve in proportion to the event that stabbed us. "Then pick up and go on." I've followed that advice most of my life, recognizing the chasm between grieving a death and a rejected manuscript. *Take time to feel the pain, but don't stay there forever. It's the way to eventually heal.*

Still, we don't need to recover immediately. Life might only allot months or days or minutes before we *must* act, but even for moments we can give ourselves permission to feel clueless and pain full. For a prescribed or even an indefinite time, we're scriptless, and that's all right. We can stop, call a time out, breathe. Nobody else knows our prescribed path anyway, except for the One who created everything. If we can't hear him right now, he'll wait—and speak when our ears open.

---

*I will not leave you as orphans;*
*I will come to you.*

—JOHN 14:18

# The Reality Gap

*In the difficult are the friendly forces,*
*the hands that work on us.*
—RAINER MARIA RILKE

Life is difficult."

In the 1980s M. Scott Peck introduced his best-selling book with that brief statement. The treatise sold wildly, but when a friend tried to read *The Road Less Traveled,* she sampled those three words and shelved the book indefinitely in her office. She didn't want to ingest that truth; wasn't sure if she ever could. It sounded too disappointing.

I don't think she ever read the book.

In defense of my friend, she'd already weathered tough times, and considering her circumstances, I wouldn't wish any more disappointment on her. She needed comfort. But she'd also confess that something in her didn't want to accept that our good expectations about life, about ourselves, don't always pan out. We fail. People hurt us. Circumstances shift beyond our control. Life is difficult.

I really didn't want to own that truth, either, but because I'm sometimes masochistic, I devoured the whole book and got depressed. My friend and I had reached our early thirties, the life era when childhood dreams develop fissures and crack a little. We didn't want to discover that gaps might occur between our expectations and reality, that a broken world can't serve us the perfection we crave. But the cracks widened without our consent anyway, and there we were, falling.

Now, the positive slant on hitting bottom is there's nowhere else to travel but up. (I know that's a cliché, but it's still true.) And that's God's encouragement to us. King David sang about the Lord: "He lifted me out of the slimy pit, out of the mud and mire; he set my feet on a rock and gave me a firm place to stand" (Psalm 40:2). A later psalm claims that, after God hoists us up, he crowns us with love and compassion (103:4).

It's hard to imagine. When we're the slimiest, the majestic King of heaven rolls up his royal sleeves, muddies himself, and extracts us from a mess. It's even more incredulous when we dig the hole, jump in feet first, and create the accident ourselves. But regardless of how we slide in, Scripture claims that God's long, rescuing arm grabs us tight, stands us on solid ground and steadies our gooped-up feet, then positions a symbol of his enduring love on our heads. It's quite a sight.

Granted, the full emergency operation may not finish as quickly as we prefer—sometimes it's years—or it may not look, feel, sound, or smell as we'd imagined. But we can lean on the Bible's promise that God wants to rescue and restore us. No matter how dark the night, no matter how deep the pit.

So what can we do? First we admit we're in a pit, that we've fallen into the reality gap and can't climb out. That's not so difficult, though. We only need to glance around and describe the surroundings, even if they're pitch black. Then we face up and start yelling.

---

*I call on the LORD in my distress,*
*and he answers me.*

—PSALM 120:1

# Where Is God?

## *A Prayer for the Perplexed*

As the deer pants for streams of water,
so my soul pants for you, O God.
My soul thirsts for God, for the living God.
When can I go and meet with God?
My tears have been my food
day and night,
while men say to me all day long,
"Where is your God?"
These things I remember
as I pour out my soul;
how I used to go with the multitude,
leading the procession to the house of God,
with shouts of joy and thanksgiving
among the festive throng.

Why are you downcast, O my soul?
Why so disturbed within me?
Put your hope in God,
for I will yet praise him,
my Savior and my God.

—PSALM 42:1-5

*Handwritten margin notes:*

Desiring God

Scripture is for
the defense of our
Joy.—p. 123

Scripture is food
for our inner man
— p. 134

Would the Psalmist
attitude be
different (more joyful)
if Scripture had
been his food
instead of his tears?

# The Constancy
# of Job's Friends

*There never were in the world two opinions alike,*
*no more than two hairs or two grains.*

—Sir Thomas Browne

An old adage says there's nothing so sure as death and taxes. I disagree. The Second Coming could commence soon, with Jesus escorting us to heaven and permanently cheating death. It's also possible to earn so little money or amass enough deductions to pay no taxes. Instead, I think there's nothing so certain as people who offer their opinions when we're in trouble—to our faces and behind our backs. In other words, there's nothing so constant as the gathering of Job's friends.

When we're in pain the burgeoning clouds of opinion roll in, and usually we don't feel quick-witted enough to dodge the downpour. Most of these people mean well; others don't. After a while both sides—the doleful advisers and the caustic critics—start to sound the same. We feel drenched to the wet, shivering bone.

At the risk of mixing one more opinion into the slosh, I say dash for cover. In the first throes of difficulty, people in pain don't need foes—or friends—wagging at them. We already know we're in trouble. It's hard to articulate the hurt. We can't yet discern all the reasons behind it (though others think they know), and because of the storm's roar, we usually can't hear anyway. Or if we do hear, we grow to resent the advice. Once a friend in trouble complained, "If I hear one more person say 'make a list and take a risk,' I'm going to puke!" She'd formed an opinion about the opinions.

However, taking cover doesn't mean we escape by ourselves, though that sounds tempting. Alone, it's too easy to self-destruct. Instead, we ask a few grace givers to join us under the proverbial canopy. Perhaps a trusted friend who'll just listen, a loved one who'll soothe us, or a therapist who'll help us think straight and take action after the initial pain subsides. The exact profiles or number of confidants doesn't matter as much as their ability not to inflict more pain with their words. Even if we're in trouble because of our sin, if we're remorseful and repentant, we need those who'll extend forgiveness, not bash us with their Bibles.

Better yet, if we're fortunate we'll take somebody under cover who'll sit in silence with us. Job's friends squatted on the ground with him for seven days and nights, without uttering a word, "for they saw that his grief was very great" (Job 2:13, NKJV). At least they grieved with him before offering their pontifications for the next thirty-five chapters.

If we've never grieved deeply, it's difficult to understand the comfort in silence and the agony of thoughtless words. I learned this at age twenty when my father died. Within hours after Dad's death, our pastor smugly strolled into the living room and chastened my mother: "God took your husband because he wouldn't become a Christian." On the other hand, my friend's parents, who'd only met my father once, stood sadly by Mom at the funeral home. After whispering condolences, the couple lingered in silence for the evening, at times squeezing Mother's hand and casting her compassionate looks. They attended a church our pastor didn't approve of, but they comforted Mom more than everyone else combined. Almost three decades later she still speaks gratefully about this couple's silence.

I'm not saying with these stories that words can't soothe us. Rather, I'm suggesting we limit our listeners and advisors when the pain descends, then widen the circle as we heal and can grasp the good intentions. This requires choosing our companions, or asking someone to sort them for us. If we straggle from person to person, spreading our sorrow like manure on a vegetable garden, we'll reap both the stench and the sprouts. I've learned that from years of repeatedly falling into trouble myself and complaining to anyone who'd listen. I also know that the sooner we forgive our critics, the faster we'll heal.

But what about the mud throwers, the ones who intentionally hurt us? My advice is to minimize their influence as much as possible, avoid slinging back at them, and beg God for a compassionate heart. When both the pagans and religious authorities mutilated Jesus with their words, he didn't reply. When the Savior hung on a cross, he agonized, "Father, forgive them, for they do not know what they are doing" (Luke 23:34). As incredulous as Christ's responses seem to our revengeful hearts, he remains our unchanging example. He expresses God the Father's desire for us in adversity.

More than anything, we can remember that God dwells under grace's canopy with us. He's our comforter, healer, guide, and deliverer. We can throw all our anxiety and sorrow on his shoulders because he loves us (1 Peter 5:7). He's the faithful Friend.

---

*Let us not love with words or tongue*
*but with actions and in truth.*

—1 JOHN 3:18

# Time for a Miracle

*A miracle...is not so much a breach*
*of the laws of nature, but rather*
*a remarkable or exceptional occurrence*
*which brought an undeniable sense*
*of the presence and power of God.*

—CHARLES HAROLD DODD

I tight-fisted my stack of bills, stepped into the dining room, and fanned them out on the hardwood floor. Then without straightening up I lowered myself physically and spiritually to lie across them, spread out like a skydiver in free-fall formation.

"Oh, God," I croaked. "These are my unpaid bills. The rent is due tomorrow. If you don't come through and help me pay them, I'm sunk." I felt anxiety's weight pinning me to the woodwork as I lay prone for at least an hour, whimpering on and off. Then I slept, fitfully.

Not long after I lost my magazine job, I sensed God calling me to work as a freelance author. I'd known that someday I would write for a living, but I didn't expect to begin this soon, this way. I thought I'd be married with a husband to support me, or that some other phantom would meet my financial needs. After prayer and consultation I felt sure of God's guidance and plunged in, carving out an income in a financial climate that's rocky for most writers. The first year passed comfortably, due to consistent consulting work along with book contracts. But on a cash-flow graph, the years since then mimic a roller coaster. Sometimes prosperous highs, mostly heart-pounding lows.

However, there's nothing quite as potent as insufficient funds to shove a person toward God. Earlier that night I'd called a friend and dumped out my worries. Fear gripped me and I sought consolation and advice.

"Read about King Hezekiah," said Anne. "The enemy backed him into a corner and God rescued him. Spread out those papers and pray the king's prayer."

I looked up 2 Kings 18-19 and found Hezekiah in a life-and-death confrontation with the King of Assyria, a horrible, Jew-demolishing enemy. This evil king sent word to Hezekiah that he'd better surrender; the Assyrian army was marching against Jerusalem, intending to slaughter everyone in that city.

"On what are you basing your confidence? Certainly the Lord won't deliver you," taunted the enemy outside the mammoth walls that once sheltered David and Solomon. "In fact, God told me to destroy you!" The Assyrian commander also terrorized the people within earshot. "Don't believe what Hezekiah says about trusting God. The Lord won't deliver you. Make peace with us or you'll die." Then echoing the Lord's admonition to the Israelites years before, he yelled, "Choose life and not death!"

King Hezekiah tore his clothes and donned sackcloth in the Lord's temple. He laid the Assyrian king's letter before God and prayed: "O LORD, God of Israel, enthroned between the cherubim, you alone are God over all the kingdoms of the earth. You have made heaven and earth. Give ear, O LORD, and hear; open your ears, O LORD, and see; listen to the words...sent to insult the living God.... Now, O LORD our God, deliver us from [the Assyrian king's] hand, so that all kingdoms on earth may know that you alone, O LORD, are God" (2 Kings 19:15-16,19). That night the Lord's angel killed 185,000 soldiers in the Assyrian camp. The enemy king withdrew and later his sons murdered him as he worshiped in a false god's temple.

Before I prayed face down on the floor, I'd read Hezekiah's plea to the Lord. With no human way out, the ancient king depended on God's deliverance. If the Lord's angel finished off thousands of armed men, perhaps he could also pay invoices. Hezekiah's prayer looked worth a try.

The next day I received an unexpected check and the rent got paid. With time, so did the other bills.

◼    ◼    ◼

"It's too bad that a smart woman like her chooses to live that way. Such a pity."

Comments like this usually point to somebody who doesn't try living up to her potential. But I know that, from fear or pride, these chilling words have been hurled at me. I've thought about this limited outlook, this misunderstanding of a writer's "unconventional" lifestyle. I wouldn't naturally choose this approach to life, but I know God called me, and with that foundation I persevere. Not with great faith or aplomb, but with the Lord's mercies and deliverances I keep writing. To be honest, the only other choice would be to exist merely, outside of God's will.

Consequently, I can think of only two situations in which to pity me. First, if I fail to follow God's purpose for me. Second, if I don't recognize difficulty as an opportunity for God to work, spinning some of his everyday miracles. I embraced the first principle easily because I love authorship, with all its quirks and sensibilities. But I'm still learning the second one, which is hard won for most everybody.

When pain and hardship strike, with Hezekiah we can say, "It's time for another one of God's miracles." Even if we feel faithless and terrified, we can still claim this because it's spiritual truth. (See Psalm 91:14; Isaiah 46:4; Jeremiah 20:13.) The Lord rescues his children—from lurking danger, the devouring devil, gnawing poverty, wounding relationships, and other corners we back into. He doesn't eke out everyday miracles to his most holy followers or those with the most horrid problems. He loves and wants to deliver us all, either from the situation or from our pain and codependency. Pity the Christian who doesn't learn that.

---

*You are the God who performs miracles;*
*you display your power among the peoples.*

—Psalm 77:14

# Fragile, Flawed, Frustrated

*The acknowledgment of our weakness*
*is the first step in repairing our loss.*
—Thomas à Kempis

You're so selfish! You never listen to what I say! I've done all this work for you, and you don't even care!"

"Oh, yeah? Well, you're just too demanding! Everybody says you're awfully hard to work for!"

"Don't throw that *everybody* stuff at me! I *dare you* to name names!"

Two angry, accusatory voices ricocheted down the office halls, and one of them was mine.

I'd known this committee meeting might be difficult, but I hadn't expected the surprising detour it took, leaving me caught off guard and defenseless. For the last hour of the agenda, I'd felt my anger building toward the chairperson and barely managed to stave it off. But now, with everybody gone but us, we verbally ripped into each other like wildcats hungry for blood.

So much for my professionalism. It was the worst fight of my life: a yelling, fist-pounding confrontation, and I felt too tired, too over-worked, to care about how this battle might damage me, my coworker, and our relationship. That is, until I tossed in bed that night, tearfully blinking at the darkness while the self-accusations arrived like mocking apparitions. *Why in the world did I behave that way? I must be a horrible person to yell like that. What's wrong with me?*

It's been said "adversities do not make the person either weak or strong, but they reveal what he is."[2] That's not a comforting thought

when inward pressures spew into volatile reactions. When we're hurting, it's even more painful to lose control and not act the way we really
want to, but that's usually what happens. In the throes of difficulty, we
may not blast a colleague, but we still might be angry, depressed, with-
drawn, critical, controlling, self-pitying, oversensitive, and all-around
hard to live with. We could also be tempted toward thoughts, habits,
addictions, and other behaviors we'd presumably conquered. Or discover some annoying personal traits we hadn't noticed before. We spend
our days feeling fragile, flawed, frustrated.

Unbelievably, it's a beneficial place to roam, at least for a season.
Ensconced in the comfort of everyday rhythms, we usually don't peer
inside and greet our imperfections. In contrast, pressure surfaces the
character and behavior patterns that God wants to root up. Wilhelm
Grimm, the compiler of ancient fairy tales, described the mythic element of stories as "small pieces of a shattered jewel which are lying
strewn on the ground all overgrown with grass and flowers, and can
only be discovered by the far-seeing eye."[3] This description also fits sinful human nature, which forms a tangled web of hidden gems and overgrown weeds. The Lord wants to pull out the weeds so the gems can
shine in clear view.

Pain that erupts into self-awareness helps us admit that we need
weeding, and generally God doesn't work deeply until we acknowledge
our weaknesses to ourselves, then to him. He could dig around without
permission because he's omniscient and powerful, but as with granting
forgiveness, he waits for our confession, sprung from a willing spirit.
Pain makes us willing.

It's not that God decides, "Now I'm going to inflict this person and
make him miserable." (He reserved that privilege for Job.) But when life
torments us—when we torment ourselves—God longs to scoop us up
in comfort, then heal both our recent and longtime sins and wounds.
We abort his loving intentions if we only accept the consolation
and reject the healing process—and eventually our refusal hurts us even

more. The wounds deepen and spread like strangling inner tentacles, and so does the pain.

David explained, "Before I was afflicted I went astray, but now I obey your word" (Psalm 119:67). One "answer" for pain is that God uses it to transform and lead us toward righteousness. But the accompanying question is: Will we let him?

---

*You hear, O LORD, the desire of the afflicted;*
*you encourage them, and you listen to their cry.*

—PSALM 10:17

# Traveling Light

## Jamie Buckingham

There are three kinds of people in the Middle East wilderness. The hermits move in from the outside, settle in caves, and stay in one place until they die. The Bedouin are nomads, on the move but always in a circle. However, God never intends for his children to settle in the wilderness as hermits or nomads. We are thus to be the third breed of wilderness person—the pilgrim. Each wilderness becomes a pilgrimage—an experience in which we meet, know, and follow God to his land of promise.

The process is simple, although often painful.

The chemist, the Holy Spirit, takes the elements of our lives and drops them into the mortar of the wilderness setting. Then, using the circumstances as a pestle, he crushes our natural elements until they come into union with each other. Pouring that fine dust into a crucible, he turns up the heat until all the impurities burst into tiny flames and disappear, leaving behind the purified self, perfectly integrated, ready for service—working all things together for good.

This is never a static process. It always involves change and progress from one state to another. It can be done only on the move.

To some degree, all of life on earth is a wilderness experience. As surely as sparks fly upward, Job pointed out, we are born into trouble. But the wilderness is a passage through trouble, not a place to stop and wallow in our adversity. As the old spiritual says, "This world is not my home, I'm just a-passin' through."

Every road sign on our trek through the wilderness of this mortal life points toward a glorious consummation of life eternal with God. We are not born to die; we are born to be reborn and live forever. As we move toward that heavenly experience, which awaits all the saints, we pass through trouble, adversity, grief, pain and hardships—all wilderness experiences. But these deserts are not designed to choke the life from us; rather, they are designed to mold us and shape us into the image of Christ. We are not ever to allow ourselves to become desert settlers like the hermits of old, or even the Bedouin of today. We are pilgrims, "a-passin' through."

■　　■　　■

Life is designed by God as a pilgrimage composed of many wildernesses. God is forever saying to all of us, "Travel light." Do not stop to build monuments. Do not overload yourself with sentimental memorabilia that ties the heartstrings to things of the past. Do not stake your sections of land as "sacred" and declare you cannot leave them behind. If you have precious belongings, send them ahead. For Jesus said, "Where your treasure is, there your heart will be also" (Matthew 6:21).

I still shudder when I recall the half-sneer, half-laugh from a Jewish archeologist when I asked her about Jewish shrines. "We Jews do not build shrines," she said. "Only Christians stop to do that. We worship a God who is on the move."

It is one of the important lessons of the desert: Keep moving! The pilgrim who pauses too long in any one place dies. Even the Bedouin, who seem bound like Prometheus to the rock of their wilderness wanderings, realize they must keep on the move. The Bedouin, though, are not pilgrims. They are nomads, wandering with the seasons in circles, with no Promised Land to beckon them onward. They are the prototype of spiritual squatters who camp smugly at a certain point of tradition or doctrine—while the winds of God's Spirit blow past.

There is the story of the hermits who fled to the desert during the fourth and fifth centuries. Monks, recluses, they moved out of the mainstream of life and never returned. Mistakenly, they thought the cloud had come to rest over them permanently.

Their pilgrimage, as they saw it, was inner. They [remained stationary] to take an inward journey to personal salvation. But in the process they stagnated. Instead of becoming servants, they become dependent upon others more practical and utilitarian to serve them. Eventually—like the Dead Sea which receives but never gives—some became mad parasites and died. And while a few indeed come face-to-face with God, most hermits remain tragic examples in history of pilgrims who view the clouds as stationary.

We must learn a lesson from the hermits, though it be a negative one. We are never called to enter a wilderness to find God, which is the essence of religion. Rather, when circumstances force us into the wilderness, we should have faith to believe God will take the initiative and reveal himself to us in his time and place. Our responsibility is to respond, and stay under the cloud as it moves to God's destined purpose for our lives.

To view the wilderness as an end—a place of abiding, rather than a place through which one passes on his way to the land of promise—is the greatest of tragedies. Since God never intended his children to enter a wilderness and remain, each wilderness experience should be accompanied by a sense of nagging dissatisfaction, a deep longing for the Promised Land to come. Pilgrims should be careful not to try to escape the suffering God places on his children, until the object of that suffering is complete. At the same time, they should arise every morning and look upward—expecting, yes, knowing, that one day the cloud will move.

*—A Way Through the Wilderness, 1983*

# That Annoying Thing Called Hope

*The very least you can do in your life
is to figure out what you hope for.
And the most you can do
is live inside that hope.
Not admire it from a distance
but live right in it, under its roof.*

—BARBARA KINGSOLVER

A medical doctor told Opal not to get pregnant again because she needed a hysterectomy. But for reasons beyond her understanding, the mother of two daughters risked another pregnancy that landed her in bed for several months so she wouldn't lose the baby forming within. Despite these efforts, the child gasped into life—and soon after barely occupied an incubator—two months ahead of her delivery date. The hand-sized daughter weighed less than four pounds and outstayed her mother's hospital enrollment. Every day after Opal's discharge from the hospital, she checked on the infant's progress.

"It was awful, feeling afraid that she wouldn't survive," Opal remembered. "But I kept hoping and praying that God would let her live." The young mother stretched her faith, and a month later she cradled a healthy baby at home. "Somehow I knew that God wanted me to have my baby, that he had something for her to do," she added.

I believe that, despite all odds, God places hope in our hearts for divine purposes. And if we cling to it, we'll reap priceless spiritual development and the fulfillment of his promises to us. Why do I believe the odds fall in our favor? I'm Opal's third daughter.

※        ※        ※

When life challenges us, we need hope to fight back. Opal reminds us that, although hope isn't tangible, it inhabits the human spirit. It's God's gift to keep us gasping, inching, battling for our lives when we're pressed by confusion or adversity or disappointment or an impossible dream. In fact, hope flourishes in the hard times. Scripture says, "We also exult in our tribulations, knowing that tribulation brings about perseverance; and perseverance, proven character; and proven character, hope; and hope does not disappoint, because the love of God has been poured out within our hearts through the Holy Spirit who was given to us" (Romans 5:3-5, NASB).

Yet hope isn't something we muscle up. Rather, it's the outflow of God's love in human hearts. If we're without hope we can ask him to renew it, just as he revives the Holy Spirit's flutterings within us. Hope never banishes second chances. Without hope, people perish. With God's hope, they believe beyond themselves.

Still, sometimes hope annoys us. We want to quit rather than fight forward, but hope can spring up in spite of our feelings. The Old Testament book of Hosea presents a stunning picture of hope that appears ridiculous to outsiders, but propels its recipient through preposterous circumstances. Obeying God's instructions, the prophet Hosea marries Gomer, a woman with a shady sexual reputation, and she bears him three children. But does Gomer appreciate this redemptive love for her, the provision of a respectable life? No, she abandons Hosea and commits adultery.

Can you image this husband's shame, the temptation to punish his wife? According to Jewish law, it'd be legal to publicly divorce her, even expected by his revengeful friends and family. But hope stirs Hosea, and he lovingly buys back his wife. She has either sold herself into slavery or prostitution, and the fee to redeem her is pitifully small. Gomer isn't worth much to anyone, except her forgiving spouse, who pays the price as if he'd purchased a princess. Hosea leads Gomer home and pampers her as if she'd always been loving, faithful, and appreciative.

God may not ask us to sustain a hope as wild as Hosea's, but then again, he might. Hope shapes differently in each person's life. It depends on God's work in us as individuals. The common denominator is that he infuses his hope into our souls, whether it's for an agnostic spouse, a wayward child, a miraculous healing, or any number of our heart's desires. Hope is the stream that washes away the past and carries us forward into God's will and goodness. As modeled by Hosea, hope in the tough times represents God's unending desire for his children.

So whatever the problem, whatever chaos swirls around or within, ask God for hope. It's rest for the soul, for "no one whose hope is in [him] will ever be put to shame" (Psalm 25:3).

---

*Let us hold unswervingly to the hope we profess,*
*for he who promised is faithful.*

—HEBREWS 10:23

# PART TWO

# Into the Shadow

When hardship splays our souls, God places us in the shadow of his hand to comfort, guide, and transform us. Nestled in the shadow, we can focus on God's love, goodness, and care during difficult times, countering the idea that he's mad at us, trying to punish us, or has abandoned us.

However, God does use trials to reshape his children, molding us into the image of Christ and collapsing the sinful habits and attitudes blocking our spirit's vitality. He hovers over us during the pain of change. We grow to understand that, instead of trapping us, the shadow of God's hand matures us for spiritual freedom and service.

# The Hovering Shadow

*Even in terrible circumstances and calamities,*
*in matters of life and death,*
*if I sense that I am in the shadow of God,*
*I find light, so much light*
*that my vision improves dramatically.*
*I know that holiness is near.*

—KATHLEEN NORRIS

As a young girl I entertained ridiculous fears that kept my mother searching for consolations and explanations. One was my aversion to shadows, especially at night. Walking the block from a friend's yard to mine at dusk, when the streetlights switched on, I feared the shadowy bushes and fence posts, the stone-still cars and street signs. In my bedroom a ruffled lampshade's shadow cast against a wall conjured up ghosts and goblins and pinned me under the bedcovers, hardly breathing. When I looked toward the door, the shadow of a family member passing through the hall loomed lifelike and menacing. I hated the dark, too, but sometimes it felt more bearable than unpredictable shadows threatening to snatch and terrorize me. At least when darkness enveloped my room, the shadows evaporated into the blackness.

With my imagination I should be a playwright or novelist because drama and literature employ shadows to a spine-stiffening advantage. Shadows evoke tension, mystery, a foreboding event or person. They're used to portray evil, suspicion, and murder. I couldn't manage writing mysteries, though, because television reruns of Alfred Hitchcock stepping into his shadow, eerie but benign by today's standards, unsettle me. And I still easily vibrate at unfamiliar noises in the night.

Whether cast from storm clouds or unfamiliar signposts, we anticipate shadows as harrowing, but in God's usual upside-down approach, he paints a positive picture of these life-darkening images. Several psalms describe the refuge for those who hide in the shadow of God's wings. We can ask to dwell under this shadow, or God may position us there until trouble passes (Psalm 17:8; 57:1). Both the pauper and the privileged can nestle under the Lord's pinions if they belong to him (36:7; 91:1). Some find this hiding place so pleasurable they sing, despite lurking danger (63:7).

Even more remarkable, God doesn't restrict why or when we can run to him. If trouble chases us, or if we've pursued trouble ourselves, God sweeps his hurting children under his hand. For some, he pours on pure comfort. For others, he uses this hiding-away time to better mold us into his image, plucking out sin and rubbing away habits and character flaws. The prophet Isaiah wrote of hiding in the shadow of God's hand as a place of personal sharpening (Isaiah 49:2). For all, the shadow extends rest, healing, and restoration.

In light of this, we need not fear God's hand. However, we can mistakenly identify his shadow as ominous because it frequently appears during grief, hardship, disappointment, or other happenings we don't understand. We may think the darkness originates from the world or the devil when actually it's from God. Especially at first, settling under the Lord's hand can feel restricting and uncomfortable, but with time we learn to appreciate what he accomplishes in us as we reside there. If we allow God to lovingly work, we'll eventually emerge wiser, stronger, better. We'll look back and cherish the time spent in his shadow.

So if darkness hovers above, try looking up. Instead of standing in the descent of evil, we could actually be under the shadow of his hand.

---

*You are my hiding place; you will protect me from trouble*
*and surround me with songs of deliverance.*

—PSALM 32:7

# The Nearby Quiver

## F. B. Meyer

In the shadow of his hand hath he hid me, and made me a polished shaft; in his quiver hath he hid me" (Isaiah 49:2, KJV).

"In the shadow." We must all go there sometimes. The glare of the daylight is too brilliant; our eyes become injured, unable to discern the delicate shades of color, or appreciate neutral tints—the shadowed chamber of sickness, the shadowed house of mourning, the shadowed life from which the sunlight has gone.

But fear not! It is the shadow of God's hand. He is leading thee. There are lessons that can be learned only there.

The photograph of His face can only be fixed in the dark chamber. But do not suppose that He has cast thee aside. Thou art still in His quiver; He has not flung thee away as a worthless thing.

He is only keeping thee close until the moment comes when He can send thee most swiftly and surely on some errand in which He will be glorified. Oh, shadowed, solitary ones, remember how closely the quiver is bound to the warrior, within easy reach of his hand, and guarded jealously.

— *Christ in Isaiah, 1895*

# Under the Wings

## *Author Unknown*

An article in *National Geographic* several years ago provided a penetrating picture of God's wings.

After a forest fire in Yellowstone National Park, forest rangers began their trek up a mountain to assess the inferno's damage. One ranger found a bird literally petrified in ashes, perched statuesquely on the ground at the base of a tree. Somewhat sickened by the eerie sight, he knocked over the bird with a stick. When he gently struck it, three tiny chicks scurried from under their dead mother's wings.

The loving mother, keenly aware of impending disaster, had carried her offspring to the base of the tree and gathered them under her wings, instinctively knowing that the toxic smoke would rise. She could have flown to safety but refused to abandon her babies. When the blaze arrived and the heat scorched her small body, the mother remained steadfast. Because she had been willing to die, those under the cover of her wings would live.

"He will cover you with his feathers, and under his wings you will find refuge" (Psalm 91:4). Being loved this much should make a difference in your life. Remember the One who loves you and then be different because of it.

—Distributed anonymously on the Internet, 1999

# A Present Help

*God is not in the slightest degree
baffled or bewildered
by what baffles and bewilders us.
He is either a present help
or he is not much help at all.*

—J. B. PHILLIPS

Growing up in a conservative Sunday school during the 1950s and 1960s deserves a red badge of courage. Or at least a special bar added to my perfect attendance pin. Backdropped against the nation's preoccupation with communism, our teachers used the Red Scare to their spiritual advantage. They told us that if the communists took over, the Reds would throw Christians into prison, including innocent children like us. So our well-meaning teachers asked the burning question: Have you memorized enough Bible verses to take with you to the dungeon?

I knew this was important because a recent issue of our adult Sunday school paper reported the story of a man in a communist prison who'd recited Scripture to himself. This kept him sane. I read the article with my own eyes, and my grade-school brain fussed about whether I'd pass the incarceration test. Though I reigned as the Scripture Memory Queen in our tiny church, I felt certain I hadn't learned enough verses, or I'd forget the ones I'd already quoted in a Sword Drill competition. Then I'd go insane and disappoint Jesus because I couldn't witness to the pagans in my jail cell who didn't know him. I finally decided that when the Soviets threw me into the clinker, I'd recite Psalm 23 over and over. I knew that passage well, and settling on this plan helped me sleep at night.

■    ▩    ■

Christians excel at scaring themselves into submission. We wonder whether we'll survive when the next tragedy strikes or the End Times prophecies shake the world. Consequently, we think if we prepare enough, we'll somehow manage. But ultimately it's God's help that we need, and his assistance can't be "stored up" for future difficulties. Scripture describes him as "a very present help" (Psalm 46:1, KJV), not a past memory or a tucked-away insurance policy. He lives with and helps us in the present tense. He bestows grace and guidance as we need it.

I find this hard to remember when adversity descends. Usually I cry and friends receive middle-of-the-night phone calls. I also contract a case of the If Onlys. "If only I'd spent more time reading my Bible, I'd know what to do now. If only I hadn't succumbed to temptation, I'd feel better about asking God to help me. If only I'd prayed longer each day, I might have staved this off."

Maybe, maybe not.

At this point it's futile to fuss about what we should have done. If we're in crisis we need help immediately, and if we cry out to God he'll hear and respond (Psalm 10:17). Even if we've sinned, God restores our relationship with him when we repent, as if we'd never left him at all (Isaiah 59:20). That sounds simplistic, but the Old Testament history of the Jews repeatedly proves the Lord's desire to extend mercy, forgiveness, and restoration to sinners who call on him. "I have seen his ways, but I will heal him; I will guide him and restore comfort to him," says God (Isaiah 57:18).

Of course, we're better off not to sin, because it bears consequences, and consistent time with God in his Word and prayer fortifies the soul. But if we need God's assistance it's not necessary or helpful to turn legalistic. The Lord says, "Run to my strong tower," (see Proverbs 18:10), and we're foolish if we don't stagger toward him. He's our first and only defense against onslaught.

Hopefully, when we cloister in God's fortress, we'll shore up our spiritual habits, realizing we might have handled this dilemma better if we'd spent more time with him—and we'll develop a holy desire and consistency that gleams after the storm passes. In that regard an encroaching problem could be the catalyst for drawing closer to God. But, in the meantime, don't worry about feeling unholy and unworthy. Scramble, limp, crawl, or claw to his safe place now.

------

*In my distress I called to the LORD;*
*I cried to my God for help.*
*From his temple he heard my voice;*
*my cry came before him, into his ears.*

—PSALM 18:6

# Broken Down

*Brokenness and wounding do not occur*
*in order to break human dignity,*
*but to open the heart so God can act.*

—MARTIN MARTY

In the film *One True Thing,* based on Anna Quindlen's novel, twenty-four-year old Ellie moves from New York City to a small town to assist her dying mother, Katherine. The daughter disdains her mother's satisfaction as a homemaker, and Ellie resents abandoning a thriving career because of a middle-aged woman's cancer. Everything in the family home, magnificently and enthusiastically created by Katherine, smacks of a life that Ellie doesn't want, from the colorful quilts to the embroidered pillows to the oil paintings of each child, now grown and living away from home.

However, as Ellie assumes the vacant wifely role—cooking, cleaning, errand running, decorating for the holidays, tending to her father's needs, and other chores—she gains an appreciation for her mother's motivations. Katherine's domestic busyness has spilled from a love and service to those whom she cherishes. At the beginning of the novel, which at times differs from the screenplay, Ellie describes herself as "still my old self, smug, self-involved, successful, and what in my circles passes for happy."[4] That description also fits the film's Ellie. However, over the next months, she transforms, sometimes with inner kicking and screaming, sometimes with outright hostility, into a different young woman. The life-altering crisis opens her eyes to what really matters and how she needs to change herself, her values, and relationships.

Like Ellie, we fear and fight our lives breaking down. Calamity hurts, and the pain can last longer than what seems bearable. It stretches and cracks, hammers and shatters, until we're broken apart and what's inside spills out. In the *One True Thing* novel, Teresa, the nurse who assists in caring for Katherine in death's last stages, explains to Ellie: "Illness brings out different qualities in different people. Some are enriched by it—yes, I know, you do not want to consider the possibility, but it's true, and I have seen it. Some people have a talent for it and some rise to the occasion. And some are diminished by their fear. They often deny, withdraw."

Later Teresa adds, "Suffering transforms."

Ellie counters that suffering sucks.

"I agree. With both conclusions, actually," the nurse replies.[5]

Brokenness transforms us, but most of us don't naturally want to accept the breaking process. That's understandable because suffering also sucks life from us. It tears from us the people or things we most adore. For Ellie, it's her mother. She realizes too late that this woman means more to her than anyone in the world. Ellie's mom feels the most personal brokenness of all: the demise of her body. But losing a child, a friend, a spouse, is devastating, too. Who can say which ranks as the worst? The degree of pain is personal; nobody can legislate how we feel. My mother says losing a child would feel the worst, though when my father died, it took years for her to begin healing, and I don't think the recovery will finish on earth. However, Mom endures physical sufferings and emotional downturns as she enters her eighties and her body systematically betrays her. It's frightening for Mom and her children. Losing our mother will feel like the worst so far.

These are the people losses, the brokenness we rarely can affect. In addition, we usually can't control sufferings that emerge from job layoffs, world events, governmental decisions, forces of nature, or sins that others commit. Or from disease, disabilities, and accidents. In other words, at times we're broken and it's not our fault. We just inadvertently stood in the path of something mightier than we are. It's the horrible price of living in a disjointed world full of factions and fallouts, the cost of original sin.

■    ■    ■

Other types of brokenness dismantle us, the kind that we contribute to either willfully or unintentionally, as if we wielded a sledgehammer and bloodied ourselves. These are the human-nature blunders, the actions we sometimes can't explain—the neglects, addictions, rebellions, wrong decisions, and stupid mistakes. They're the follies of youth, the digressions of our middle years, the misperceptions of old age, and all the missteps in between. We wince at these errors and ask, "What in the world was I thinking?" and pay therapists to help us answer that question. Through these we admit that Scripture tells the truth: We're fools when we make choices without God. Self-inflicted brokenness carries a peculiar pain, full of regret and guilt and more questions that may subside for a while, but flare up with a memory, a temptation, or someone's innocent comments or deliberate revenge, like diabetic sores that resist permanent healing.

In my forty-something years, I've splattered around an assortment of mistakes, but the most regretful spillages have been the stains that, no matter how hard I try, can't be blotted from someone's heart. I don't like offending people, especially when my actions cause them to dislike me, but I've usually managed to confess my sin, forsake it, and plod forward, discarding my worries about the past. But this year I've smashed into what feels like an unending, unalterable unforgiveness from somebody who won't accept apologies or let others forget my mistake. A white-hot anger spews at me through unrepeatable words, unleashing years of hidden resentment, based on opinions about my life that barely resemble the truth. My close friends know the real me and believe this person spins out of control. But this person is not an individual I can escape, so the pain doesn't fully heal. Sometimes it feels there are no resources left for defending myself, little that's tangible to bolster my emotional equilibrium.

Interestingly, my offense wasn't against this person. I sinned against someone else who forgave me and wants to put it behind us, but an onlooker has become the avenger who thinks I've dealt blithely with the matter. This person hasn't acknowledged my tears and regret and repenting, and has bludgeoned my reputation before people who matter to me. Scripture says God makes all things work together for his good, but for now accomplishing the tasks of an ordinary day is the miracle, though it's not apparent to most people. The brokenness aches inside.

As with anything that's broken, we might function nominally when we're suffering, or stop altogether like splintered cogs or scattered shards, facedown, useless, and abandoned. But God doesn't forsake us. He cradles us in his hands, stroking our listless limbs and pressing his face against ours so we hear his soothing promise: "Can a mother forget the baby at her breast and have no compassion on the child she has borne? Though she may forget, I will not forget you!" (Isaiah 49:15).

Not only does God comfort us; he participates in our brokenness. However the shattering originates, he melts the pieces and refashions us into more spiritually pliable but durable vessels. "Remove the dross from the silver, and out comes material for the silversmith," wrote Solomon (Proverbs 25:4), who surrounded himself with the choicest vessels in the world, but also felt the spiritual sluggishness of dross in his soul. But more important, brokenness can fully open us to God, illuminating the soul's dark places.

In his book, *The Journey of Desire,* John Eldredge describes God as the divine thwarter. Sometimes the Lord thwarts our plans so he can unearth the idols we've buried inside. Described another way, God breaks us to expose our sin so we can forsake it. I believe God wants to accomplish both of these intents—to spotlight sin and strengthen me—in my brokenness. But it's hard for me to marry the concept of a loving God to the Thwarter who also breaks us. I repeatedly need him to teach me the value of true and corrective love.

Gratefully, even when the Lord thwarts us, he promises not to break us forever. (See Isaiah 28:23-29.) We're only on the threshing floor long enough to loosen the chaff, the superficial encasements in our lives, from the wheat, the particles of value and sustenance, then toss the debris to the winds. And there's good reason to endure and cooperate, to lie on the hard, dirt-pounded surface until he finishes. If the chaff doesn't fall away, we might be threshed again or discarded for use altogether. So this time I want to get it right, to understand and endure this difficult process until the worthless winnows away. Then perhaps, at last, I'll emerge with eternity's One True Thing stamped on my heart.

---

*The sacrifices of God are a broken spirit;*
*a broken and contrite heart,*
*O God, you will not despise.*

—PSALM 51:17

# Turn to Me, Lord

## *A Prayer for the Lonely*

To you, O LORD, I lift up my soul;
in you I trust, O my God....

Turn to me and be gracious to me,
for I am lonely and afflicted.
The troubles of my heart have multiplied;
free me from my anguish.
Look upon my affliction and my distress
and take away all my sins.
See how my enemies have increased
and how fiercely they hate me!
Guard my life and rescue me;
let me not be put to shame,
for I take refuge in you.
May integrity and uprightness protect me,
because my hope is in you.

—PSALM 25:1-2,16-21

# In Good Hands

## *Fiction by Hannah Hurnard*

They reached the desert surprisingly quickly, although the path was very steep indeed. Much-Afraid was leaning on the Shepherd, and did not feel her weakness at all. By the evening of that same day, they were down on the pale sand dunes and walking toward some huts built in the shadow of one of the great pyramids, where they were to rest that night. At sunset, when the sky burned fiery red over the western rim of the desert, the Shepherd led Much-Afraid away from the huts, to the foot of the pyramid....

In the morning the Shepherd called Much-Afraid again and led her away, but this time he opened a little door in the wall of the pyramid and took her inside. There was a passage which led to the center, and from there a spiral staircase went up to the floors above.

But the Shepherd opened another door leading out of the central chamber on the ground floor and they entered a very large room which looked like a granary. There were great piles of grain everywhere except in the middle. There on the open space men were threshing the different kinds of grain in many different ways and then grinding them into powder, some coarse and some fine. At one side were women sitting on the ground with hollow smooth stones before them, grinding the very best of the wheat into the finest possible powder.

Watching them for a while, Much-Afraid saw how the grains were first beaten and bruised until they crumbled to pieces, but still the grinding and beating process continued, until at last the powder was fine enough to be used for baking the best wheat bread.

"See," said the Shepherd gently, "how various are the methods used for grinding the different varieties of grain, according to their special use and purpose." Then he quoted, "Dill is not threshed with a threshing instrument, neither is a cart wheel turned about upon cummin; but dill is beaten out with a staff, and the cummin with a rod. Bread corn is bruised, but no one crushes it forever; neither is it broken with the wheel of a cart not bruised with horsemen driving over it" (Isaiah 28:27-28, KJV [*sic*]).

As Much-Afraid watched the women pounding the bread corn with their heavy stones she noticed how long the process took before the fine white powder was ready for use. Then she heard the Shepherd saying, "I bring my people into Egypt that they, too, may be threshed and ground into the finest powder and may become bread corn for the use of others. But remember, though bread corn is bruised, no one threshes it forever; only until the bruised and broken grain is ready for its highest use. 'This also cometh forth from the Lord of hosts, which is wonderful in counsel, and excellent in working'" (verse 29, KJV).

After this the Shepherd took her back to the central chamber and they ascended the spiral staircase, twisting up and up into the darkness above. There, on the next floor, they came to another and smaller room, in the center of which stood a great wheel, flat like a table. Beside it stood a potter who wrought a work on the wheel. As he spun the wheel he fashioned his clay into many beautiful shapes and objects. The material was cut and kneaded and shaped as he saw fit, but always the clay lay still upon the wheel, submitting to his every touch, perfectly, unresisting.

As they watched, the Shepherd said, "In Egypt, too, I fashion my fairest and finest vessels and bring forth instruments for my work, according as I see fit." (see Jeremiah 18:4, KJV). Then he smiled and added, "Cannot I do with you, Much-Afraid, as this potter? Behold, as 'clay in the hand of the potter, so are you in my hand'" (verse 6)....

◾   ◾   ◾

Last of all he took her up the stairway to the highest floor. There they found a room with a furnace in which gold was being smelted and refined of all its dross. Also in the furnace were rough pieces of stone and rock containing crystals. These were put in the great heat of the oven and left for a time. On being taken out, behold, they were glorious jewels, flashing as though they had received the fire into their very hearts. As Much-Afraid stood beside the Shepherd looking shrinkingly into the fire, he said the loveliest thing of all.

"O thou afflicted, tossed with tempest, and not comforted, behold, I will lay thy stones with fair colours, and lay thy foundations with sapphires. And I will make thy windows of agates, and thy gates of carbuncles, and all thy borders of pleasant stones" (Isaiah 54:11-12, KJV). Then he added, "My rarest and choicest jewels and my finest gold are those who have been refined in the furnace of Egypt."...

They stayed at the huts in the desert for several days, and Much-Afraid learned many things which she never heard before.

One thing, however, made a special impression upon her. In all that great desert, there was not a single green thing growing, neither tree nor flower nor plant save here and there a patch of straggly grey cacti.

On the last morning she was walking near the tents and huts of the desert dwellers when in a lonely corner behind a wall she came upon a little golden-yellow flower, growing all alone. An old pipe was connected with a water tank. In the pipe was one tiny hole through which came an occasional drop of water. Where the drops fell one by one, there grew the little golden flower, though where the seed had come from, Much-Afraid could not imagine, for there were no birds anywhere and no other growing things.

She stooped over the lonely, lovely little golden face, lifted so hopefully and so bravely to the feeble drip, and cried out softly, "What is your name, little flower, for I never saw one like you before."

The tiny plant answered at once in a tone as golden as itself, "Behold me! My name is Acceptance-with-Joy."

Much-Afraid thought of the things which she had seen in the pyramid: the threshing-floor and the whirring wheel and the fiery furnace. Somehow the answer of the little golden flower which grew all alone in the waste of the desert stole into her heart and echoed faintly but sweetly, filling her with comfort. She said to herself, "He has brought me here when I did not want to come for his own purpose. I, too, will look up into his face and say, 'Behold me! I am thy little handmaiden Acceptance-with-Joy.'"

*—Hinds' Feet on High Places, 1977*

# The Rescuers

*Your comfort makes the rescue.*

*ANTONY AND CLEOPATRA*

I've never raised children, so my cats, Monet and Wolfie, both named after creative masterminds, catch the brunt of my latent and clumsy maternal instincts. I feel protective of them, so for a few years I denied them their natural desire to roam through the wilds, or in our case, the limited expanse of a grassy backyard. They romped inside the house.

Felines, however, possess a clever brilliance, and somehow this last year they convinced me to slide open the back door and release them, at least for a portion of each good-weather day. I don't know why I did this—maybe because I finally trust their attachment to me; I now belong to their irrevocable animal territory. Or perhaps they pattern after their namesakes, both endowed with entrancing traits that converted authority figures into followers. Or maybe it's just that I love them and wish their happiness. Cats revel in the outdoors.

Whatever the reason, it didn't take long for Wolfie to scramble up an aged ash tree that spreads its limbs over the deck, with Monet, always the imitator of his older brother, not far behind. I panicked. With only their back claws intact, how would they navigate getting down without injuries? The only limb Monet could return on required a straight vertical drop, and Wolfie's branch wavered, threatening to break under his unequipped front paws. I cajoled and fussed, clattered in the shed for a nonexistent extension ladder, and complained about their temerity. They scanned the upward possibilities and climbed higher.

As I craned my neck and yammered at my pets' selective hearing, I remembered something a longtime cat owner told me years ago, before I even liked the creatures. "Nobody has ever seen a cat skeleton in a tree. Eventually they come back down on their own terms." Now coerced into trusting the man's wisdom and practicality, I decided to recommence my chores inside the house and let the fur fall, though I also wanted to locate the veterinarian's phone number. However, as I resigned myself toward the house, I heard a rustling and glanced up in time to watch both cats defy gravity, deftly maneuvering their back paws for swift descents. Finally low enough, they lit off the trunk, landed upright with all fours on the deck, and sauntered off as if to say, "No big deal."

That's the day I determined to stop worrying about rescuing "the boys" from high places. I needed to let cats be cats. They knew how to help themselves; they didn't need my help. In fact, my intervention could have muddled their natural instincts and caused an injurious fall to the deck or sidewalk.

■   ■   ■

When hardship strikes, our closest friends and family members instinctively want to rescue us. They'd do most anything to numb the pain, climb the heights, or reroute criticism from our hearing range. Just say the word and they'll detonate the mountains we can't budge, or at least express their desire to when it's not possible.

People morph into wannabe rescuers because they love us, and these heroic intentions display their loyalty. When we're suffering we need that kind of reassurance, especially if we're hurting from self-inflicted wounds. But even if the trouble doesn't brew from our blunders, we're comforted that somebody wants to (or at least wishes he or she could) straighten up the mess. But yanking us out of trouble could be a terrible solution. Though we need our loved ones' help — even their claims that they'd solve it all for us if they could — too much actual intrusion might obscure the lessons God wants to teach us or abort the mission we're to accomplish. We need to carefully discern what advice we take, even if it offers an easy way out, even if it's from a person closely associated with us.

This doesn't mean friends and family shouldn't offer sympathy, hand us money, or "roll up their sleeves" and plow through a project with us. Loving, pragmatic assistance keeps us slogging forward, both physically and emotionally. It's a visible expression of love. Yet some well-meaning people want to obliterate our hardship for the wrong reasons. Frankly, some people want our suffering to end so it'll release them from the struggle too. They don't want to hear our groanings or bear burdens with us. Their approach to difficulty says, "Let's get this over with as fast as we can." Others don't discern how to walk the fine line between support and control, feverishly working to manipulate the situation—and us—into what they consider an acceptable outcome. But this can translate into what makes *them* feel and look best.

Others might dig for the "hidden meaning" behind our calamity, believing it's their responsibility to solve the spiritual riddle for us. They think if we would just live the *right way,* we wouldn't face these difficulties. If they can unlock the spiritual key, the suffering will end. They're ripe with messages from God and constant in their approach. One friend, concerned about my income, peered over her glasses and surmised, "Well, if a ministry is *really* from the Lord, then there's always enough money to support it. If God calls us, he also supplies what we need." She told me this three different times, knowing I'd recently wandered into a financial Sahara.

Compare that to another friend who handed me five hundred dollars and said, "I know it's tough now, but I believe God has called you to this ministry, and someday it will flourish." Both her words and donation assured me that she's in the battle with me, for as long as it lasts. She typifies the caring people who truly want what's best for us. It hurts them to watch us wrestle with our dreams and tragedies. These comforters would like to stop the madness, but they can't and they know it. We draw solace and courage from their desires, though, and that's what matters. They're wannabe rescuers, based on love instead of impatience or control or judgment. Yet at the same time, they don't want us to miss the lessons and character growth forged in the fire.

These caregivers are rare treasures. As we pick our way through the rubble, we can train our eyes to find and focus on them.

---

*If one falls down,*
*his friend can help him up.*
*But pity the man who falls*
*and has no one to help him up!*

—ECCLESIASTES 4:10

# Take This Cup

*Henri Nouwen*

Can you drink the cup that I am going to drink?" Jesus asked his friends. They answered yes, but had no idea what he was talking about. Jesus' cup is the cup of sorrow, not just his own sorrow but the sorrow of the whole human race. It is a cup full of physical, mental, and spiritual anguish. It is the cup of starvation, torture, loneliness, rejection, abandonment, and immense anguish. It is the cup full of bitterness.

Who wants to drink it? It is the cup Isaiah calls "the cup of [God's] wrath. The chalice, the stupefying cup, you have drained to the dregs" (Isaiah 51:17, NJB), and what the second angel in the book of Revelation calls "the wine of retribution" (Revelation 14:8, NJB), which Babylon gave the whole world to drink.

When the moment to drink that cup came for Jesus, he said, "My soul is sorrowful unto the point of death" (Matthew 26:38, NJB). His agony was so intense that "his sweat fell to the ground like great drops of blood" (Luke 22:44, NJB). His close friends James and John, whom he asked if they could drink the cup he was going to drink, were there with him but fast asleep, unable to stay awake with him in his sorrow. In his immense loneliness, he fell to his face and cried out, "My Father [*sic*], if it is possible, let this cup pass me by" (Matthew 26:39, NJB). Jesus couldn't face it. Too much pain to hold, too much suffering to embrace, too much agony to live through. He didn't feel he could drink that cup filled to the brim with sorrows.

Why then could he still say yes? I can't fully answer that question, except to say that beyond all the abandonment experienced in the body and mind Jesus still had a spiritual bond with the one he called Abba. He possessed a trust beyond betrayal, a surrender beyond despair, a love beyond all fears. This intimacy beyond all human intimacies made it possible for Jesus to allow the request to let the cup pass him by become a prayer directed to the one who had called him "My Beloved."

Notwithstanding his anguish, that bond of love had not been broken. It couldn't be felt in the body, nor thought through in the mind. But it was there, beyond all feelings and thoughts, and it maintained the communion underneath all disruptions. It was that spiritual sinew, that intimate communion with his Father, that made him hold the cup and pray, "My Father, let it be as you, not I, would have it" (Matthew 26:39, NJB).

Jesus didn't throw the cup away in despair. No, he kept it in his hands, willing to drink it to the dregs. This was not a show of willpower, staunch determination, or great heroism. This was a deep spiritual yes to Abba, the lover of his wounded heart.

When I contemplate my own sorrow-filled heart, when I think of my little community of people with mental handicaps and their assistants, when I see the poor of Toronto, and the immense anguish of men, women, and children far and wide on our planet, then I wonder where the great yes has to come from. In my own heart and the hearts of my fellow people, I hear the loud cry, "O God, if it is possible, let this cup of sorrow pass us by." I hear it in the voice of the young man with AIDS begging for food on Yonge street, in the little cries of starving children, in the screams of tortured prisoners, in the angry shouts of those who protest against nuclear proliferation and the destruction of the planet's ecological balance, and in the endless pleas for justice and peace all over the world. It is a prayer rising up to God not as an incense but as a wild flame.

From where then will come that great yes? "Let it be as you, not I, will have it." Who can say yes when the voice of love hasn't been heard? Who can say yes when there is no Abba to speak to? Who can say yes when there is no moment of consolation? In the midst of Jesus' anguished prayer asking his Father to take his cup of sorrow away, there was one moment of consolation. Only the Evangelist Luke mentions it. He says, "Then an angel appeared to him, coming from heaven to give him strength" (Luke 22:43, NJB).

In the midst of the sorrows is consolation, in the midst of the darkness is light, in the midst of the despair is hope, in the midst of Babylon is a glimpse of Jerusalem, and in the midst of the army of demons is the consoling angel. The cup of sorrow, inconceivable as it seems, is also the cup of joy. Only when we discover this in our own life can we consider drinking it.

*— Can You Drink the Cup? 1996*

# PART THREE

# The Crucial Struggle

When God arranges us in the shadow of his hand, we can choose to fight or cooperate with him. It's a crucial struggle and choice. Fighting blocks his work and grace in our lives and leads to further pain, disappointment, and possibly spiritual downfall. We stunt our growth emotionally and spiritually.

In contrast, cooperating with the pain allows the Holy Spirit to apply his healing balm and comfort, pouring his attributes into us. If we accept rather than reject the shadow of God's hand, it transforms from a cave of dark withdrawal into a nestling retreat.

# The Real Problem

*Problems cannot be solved at the same level*
*of awareness that created them.*

—ALBERT EINSTEIN

In the novel *The Poisonwood Bible,* author Barbara Kingsolver arrestingly unfolds the story of a Baptist family that leaves Bethlehem, Georgia, in 1960 for a one-year missionary term in the Belgian Congo. Beforehand, the father tries to explain the difference between America and Africa. "Where we are headed, there will be no buyers and sellers at all," the Reverend Nathan Price tells his wife and four daughters, ages five to fifteen. "Not so much as a Piggly Wiggly."

This comment initiates a bare-minimum contingency plan by his wife, Orleanna. In their spare bedroom the mother lays out worldly goods she thinks the family, especially the daughters, can't live without. She packs Betty Crocker cake mixes for birthdays, a dozen cans of Underwood deviled ham, an ivory plastic mirror, a stainless-steel thimble, a good pair of scissors, a dozen number-two pencils, an array of Band-Aids, over-the-counter medicines, and much more. Even the father, who acts dismayed by the process, adds to the pile: a hatchet, a latrine spade, a claw hammer, packets of vegetable seeds, a Baptist hymnal, and several Bibles.

Just when Orleanna thinks she has remembered all the necessities, she discovers that the airline allows each passenger to carry only forty-four pounds of luggage across the Atlantic Ocean. Adding up everyone's baggage weight, including the suitcase of five-year-old Ruth May who's awarded the adult allotment, the family exceeds its total limit by sixty-one pounds. After describing this dilemma to the Baptist Mission League, Orleanna learns that the airlines don't weigh passengers and takes the hint. She and her daughters leave the United States carrying their excess belongings on their bodies, under layers of clothes. According to Leah, one of the twin daughters, "My sisters and I left home wearing six pairs of underdrawers, two half-slips and camisoles; several dresses one on top of the other, with pedal pushers underneath; and outside of everything an all-weather coat.... The other goods, tools, cake-mix boxes and so forth were tucked out of sight in our pockets and under our waistbands, surrounding us in clanking armor."

The Price girls form a humorous image of resourcefulness, but unfortunately the "fun" doesn't last long. Within days and months after the family's arrival, most of what they drug to Africa doesn't translate to that culture. Cake mixes spoil in the sweltering heat, plants from Western seeds won't flower and produce food, and there's no practical need for pinking shears. In addition, Nathan Price's spiritual beliefs don't capture African hearts because he teaches (and condemns) the people of Kilanga from an American mindset, never bothering to learn and adapt to their pragmatic customs. He's too self-focused and arrogant to change. Sadly, the rest of the novel powerfully describes the unraveling of a family and the father's mental, emotional, and physical demise.

Nathan Price's downfall is that he focuses on the wrong problem. He thinks it's critical to change the people and their ways, when he first needs to examine and transform himself. It's difficult, then turns impossible, for him to be "an instrument of God's perfect will" with a devil of an attitude. So the Congo chews him up and spits him out.[6]

■　　■　　■

When we're in crisis and pain, the same misguided focus can plague us. We blame the devil, other people, and circumstances for our difficulties and spend huge amounts of time praying, plotting, and fretting about how to change them. We rail at Satan and feel sorry for quirky and sinful folks around us. But the real problem could be us. We may be in trouble because of our own self-preoccupation, religious pride, or outright sin, and God wants to change that. He longs for children who walk freely but humbly, willing to serve the world with open hands instead of trying to control it. Able to adapt without losing their spiritual center. But first, like the Price family, we need to abandon the things that hinder us, the things we cling to but really don't need.

Near the novel's conclusion, Rachel, the oldest Price daughter, says, "You can't just sashay into the jungle aiming to change it all…without expecting the jungle to change you right back."[7] Generally, we can't blame everyone and everything else without getting exposed ourselves. People and circumstances may not change, but we can. And the sooner we identify the real problem, the better life gets. When we adopt a warmer approach to people, they aren't so icy toward us. When we curb an addiction, we don't live in crisis as much. If we stop gossiping, we might gain more friends. Changing ourselves often sets in motion the principle of cause and effect.

I learned this after owning up to a lifelong struggle with depression. I'd lived with a sad or negative outlook for so long, I'd grown accustomed to the blue funks, crying jags, or tense and impatient broods that routinely settled on me. I was moody, and it confused and annoyed people. Certain relationships strained. I kept thinking if I surrendered to God more, disciplined myself better, and tried harder, I could beat the mood swings. But unfortunately, an inherited, genetic depression like mine only sinks deeper as its victim grows older. I got worse.

Eventually the troops assembled and my Waterloo commenced at the office. Some people whom I managed complained to my boss about the moodiness. He stumbled through "disciplining" me and the humiliation cut to the marrow, but I finally sought medical help. It took awhile, but eventually the depression loosened its grip. Most of the people who weathered my mood disorder forgave me, especially when they observed how I'd changed, and time erased the apprehension that

I would regress. Today, as long as I stick with the doctor's prescription, I seldom get depressed.

Still, the process dictated a disturbing, under-the-surface look at myself. Unremitting stress coerced me to discover the real irritant in my relationships, and in this case it was me. Sometimes pressure is the only instrument that coaxes change.

---

*If you really change your ways and your actions*
*and deal with each other justly...*
*then I will let you live in this place,*
*in the land I gave your forefathers for ever and ever.*

—JEREMIAH 7:5,7

# Getting Stuck

*If I stoop*
*Into a dark tremendous sea of cloud,*
*It is but for a time; I press God's lamp*
*Close to my breast; its splendor, soon or late,*
*Will pierce the gloom; I shall emerge someday.*

—ROBERT BROWNING

In my early thirties I volunteered for a women's organization that sponsored large conferences in Chicago, with the goal of introducing urbanites to Christ. Sometimes I worked with the ministry's director, a midlife woman I respected. Carol practiced an intense and abiding interaction with God. One night as we walked toward the sunset that settled on her neighborhood, she talked about ministry problems. Then she announced something that startled me. With frustration welling up from a deep soul space, she complained, "I feel stuck! God won't let me move backward or forward. I'm stuck, stuck, stuck!"

I can't remember how I replied, but I did think, *If somebody like her feels stuck, then where's the hope for a spiritual peon like me?* I needed to live longer to recognize that spiritual inertia happens to most Christians, and often repeatedly. She'd honored me with her vulnerability and unwittingly mentored my need for a spiritual reality check. Through the centuries "feeling stuck" has originated concepts such as "dark night of the soul" and wandering into a spiritual desert or wilderness. The dense atmosphere stifling our spirits stalls us, and we can't pull ourselves up and step out. Sometimes we're the lethargic culprits; other times, it feels as though God leans against us. We can feel stymied emotionally, spiritually, physically, personally, or directionally. Life constructs count-less traps to render us motionless.

It's common to feel stuck in a difficult situation, especially if grief or frustration threatens to linger indefinitely. We don't want to regress on our journey, but neither can we figure out how to progress. Either we can't develop a solution, or we can't muster enough energy to try. After a while, staying in bed feels like the best option, and I know if I begin sleeping too much I'm feeling stuck and hopeless. In the last few years, with so many disappointments flung my way, I've repeatedly felt as though I won't move forward again, and after enough discouraging hits, I'm sometimes not sure if I want to anyway. Rather than delving into problem solving, I try burrowing further into the mattress. Aside from re-plumping my pillow, it's the only movement I care to make.

At some point, however, for pride's sake or from boredom, I have to get up. I need to ask the question, "Why am I so stuck?" So far I haven't liked the probabilities, because often the underlying cause is spiritual. There's something to identify and sift through, perhaps something God wants me to learn before trekking again. But what could the lesson be? What is the barrier?

An unpalatable answer is that sometimes God hides what's ahead, insisting that we trust him in the smothering places. Here it's not the heat's energy but the perpetual motionless, the hanging out to dry in the stillness, that remakes character and deepens our spiritual life. My guess is that much "stuckness" falls into this category: The answer is that God doesn't readily provide a solution, or perhaps there's no solu-tion at all. We're to abide until, like the ancient Israelites, his pillared cloud beckons us forward. However, hardly anyone likes this explana-tion. It's no fun loitering in a sweltering desert, weary and direction-less with nothing to enliven the senses. It's tempting, even relieving for a while, to grump and complain. No wonder the Jews griped their way through the Desert of Sin. Day after day, the landscape looked blandly familiar.

A wall calendar in my kitchen quotes Marcel Proust as saying, "The real voyage of discovery consists not in seeking new landscapes, but in having new eyes." I don't know if Proust the man ever stalled in the heat, but Proust the writer did invent a sort of desert wisdom. He understood that, when we can't change our location, we can alter our way of observing it. Our surroundings may not look as monotonous as we think they do. In fact, many people lovingly call the desert their home. They'd rather weather the summer's sweat than a snowy winter's drifts, and in many cases the heat soothes arthritic bones and heals ailments. The desert teems with varieties of vegetation and wildlife, and underground streams service the thirsty.

Last August I visited my mother who'd moved to a seniors' complex in the Phoenix area a few months before. I moaned and groaned about the hundred-degree heat. "Nothing but a bunch of sand and prickly plants," I muttered. "How can she stand this?" But after a week, walking past succulent gardens every day to fetch the mail or use the laundry room, or driving past untamed public parks on my way to the grocery store, I opened my eyes to the scenery. The variety of cacti stunned me. Light, dark, variegated, stubby, elongated, smooth, ridged, prickly and flowered, ancient and new, they stood everywhere as proud statues—great works of art that only nature could create and contain. I'm a fan of many types of artwork, so when I shifted my outlook, thinking of myself visiting a vast fine arts museum with endless rooms to explore, I savored the view. Two weeks later as I drove out of town, pushing uphill toward Flagstaff and out of Arizona, I wanted to take in as much desert scenery as possible. "Good-bye, beauties," I whispered to the prickly plants. "I'm actually going to miss you."

Even the desert extends vistas that please, activities that satiate, lessons that enrich us, if we'll open our eyes to the possibilities. We might even miss them after we leave.

■    ■    ■

Perhaps an equally distasteful reason for "stuckness" is our disobedience. We haven't done what the Lord already told us to do, and he's waiting for compliance. We're participating in a cosmic stalemate and God intends to win. In the previous explanation for stuckness, we can only wait; in this instance, the choice to move remains ours. Sadly, it's possible to stay inert for a lifetime.

I recoil at mentioning this reason. We can place blame where it doesn't belong, causing sincere spiritual travelers to feel even more discouraged. I don't want to burden people with what doesn't fit them, and my spiritual gift of mercy prefers to forgive rather than point the finger. (I'd make a lousy prophet.) But I've experienced a few stalemates in my life, a stuckness that I suspect derives from pleasures I shouldn't cling to but still nurture, so I present this option—as a sinner, not as someone who's blameless. I'm banking on God's patience and grace to endure until I tire of my folly, stop skulking, and repent, not just again, but finally. I'm comforted that when Hagar escaped to the desert, God already resided there, waiting for her. She named him "the God who sees me" (Genesis 16:13).

I also resonate with Anne Lamott's admission in *Traveling Mercies* that she's "a bad born-again Christian." Anne's a believer but she's in process, not completely redeemed yet, with areas in her life that still need God's touch. Reading her book, I balk at some of the language and opinions, raw and unexpected, but from chapter to chapter I walk with a woman who's honest about her failings and search for God. However, Anne will probably always resist stereotypes, and I like that. Most biblical heroes sprang from this mold, and God walked with and sometimes chased or yanked them. I think as long as we're open to God, staying in communication with him, letting go of what's spiritually disabling, we'll eventually get unstuck.

Recently I've heard about another plausible cause for "stuckness" that intrigues me. We may harbor hidden beliefs, disguised or submerged opinions, that prevent us from being our true selves, growing as multifaceted individuals and pursuing God's good gifts. For example, we might desire marriage, but internally a voice insists, "I'm not worth loving. Everybody else deserves a partner, but not me." Or, in pursuit of God's mission for us, we privately say, "I'm not talented enough for this. I'm going to fail God and disintegrate." It's common to feel stuck during difficulty, so we add, "See! All this trouble proves that I'm terrible! A 'good person' wouldn't have so much junk to wade through. I'm never going to get out of this."

However these lies first asserted themselves—from something said or done or withheld—over the years they're intricately laced into our belief system by the soul's enemy. The handiwork is so finely detailed, so embedded within an overall design, and so long lived with and believed, we don't discern its insidious influence. Consequently, we get stuck. Desiring but doubting. Wanting but not willing to risk. Industrious but ineffective. And frustrated with a capital F.

Hidden beliefs can grow into vows that bind us or quiet curses we can't break by ourselves. But when we say, "I can't," God says, "I can." He can rupture the enemy's hold on us, silencing the hissing in our ears. But first we need to identify our hidden beliefs; the fears we keep locked in our hearts, the negative self-opinions we tell nobody else. Then we know what to ask him for so he can deliver us.

Remember that Satan wants to cement our immobility, and he'll try an exasperating number of ways to stall us. Usually I write a book entry like this in a day. I worked on this chapter for a week, repeatedly fretting and leaving it and praying and trying again. I got stuck on the chapter about feeling stuck! But as I explained earlier, God intends to win, so these pages aren't blank.

---

*Free me from the trap that is set for me,*
*for you are my refuge.*

—PSALM 31:4

# The Instant Rebel

*Paul Tournier*

I must now tackle the last theme: "the Christian's attitude to his own suffering." To accept! Acceptance is difficult. Passive reaction and resignation have no virtue. Old people who go to die in a corner are more like injured animals than human beings.

Rebellion! That is the usual reaction, and no one need be ashamed of feeling rebellious when fate strikes him. Most people hide it, but the first reaction, the normal reaction in the eyes of a psychologist or a doctor, is revolt. Open your Bible, and you will see that the greatest believers were rebels—Isaiah, Jeremiah, and all the rest. There were even movements of rebellion in Jesus himself. So do not be ashamed of rebellion. It is normal. It is necessary to be able to pass through this zone of indignation in order to reach true acceptance, not by an effort of the will, but with the present help of the Spirit.

The purpose of life is not the absence of suffering, but that the suffering should bear fruit. Jesus warned his followers that they would experience tribulation and persecution. And St. Francis said, "The good that I wait for is so great that all pain is a joy to me." That is the triumph of the Spirit and of faith which can transform suffering into the joy of knowing God more intimately.

When my younger son broke his leg, he said, "At last something's happened to me!" We had been trying so hard to protect him from every danger that he had the feeling of not really being alive. If one does not suffer, one does not live. I have seen people discovering that they were alive through the experience of suffering. It can make us cry out to God. Calvin, who suffered from stomach pains, would exclaim, in his vivid way, "Oh my God, you are grinding me!" How many of the saints have had this experience of the transformation of suffering, not in a philosophical sense, as if it were God who sent it, but in the sense of being turned by it toward God? And what can the meaning of life be, if it is not to find God?

In the book of Job, to which I have referred, there is no answer to the problem of the suffering of the righteous, though God has his thunderings and his lightnings flashing in the clouds—which rather shocked the philosopher Jung, who felt that God was in the wrong in leaving Job without an answer. In the end, however, Job meets God and says, "I knew you only by hearsay; but now I have seen you with my own eyes."

Yes, suffering can be the occasion of meeting God. I am reminded of a mother who had lost her daughter who was in the prime of her life. She came to see me and said, "From now on I have a link with heaven." So a very grievous bereavement can create a solidarity with heaven. We have one foot in heaven because our treasure is already there, and we long to rejoin it.

You understand what we are struggling for! Our aim is to help humanity look at things no longer only in their technological, external, inhuman aspect, but also to see what is at stake on the human level, in the life of every person. This is the struggle of faith which can find meaning even in suffering, in failure and amputation, and win through to intimacy with the Savior.

The heart of the gospel is not a doctrine, but a person, a suffering being. In suffering, the Christian can approach Jesus and identify with him, in his death and in his victory. The maturity of the person, the full growth of the spiritual being, does not come about without suffering, or at least without communion with the suffering of others.

Catholics employ a notion which is unfamiliar to protestants—the idea of offering up their suffering [as a sacrificial gift to God], and I think it is up to me as a protestant doctor to say that they are right. Paul speaks of his sufferings as a way of making up all that has still to be undergone by Christ. "I live now not with my own life, but with the life of Christ who lives in me," he says. This identification with Jesus is a well-known psychological phenomenon. It is called communion. Union with Jesus unites us with others in the certainty that the supreme hope is beyond this world, in a new earth and a new order where, as the book of Revelation says, there will be no more death, and no more mourning or sadness.

*—A Listening Ear, 1987*

# Yelling at God

Habakkuk yelled at God and lived to write about it. Actually, I think anyone blessed with the name *Habakkuk* deserves to scream, but the prophet squandered no time wailing about personal injustices. Much larger, more urgent issues consumed him. He complained to the Lord about the sin in Judah, the Jewish southern kingdom. "Why do you allow evil in this land?" he asked. "Why don't you listen to me when I call for help?"

Exasperated, Habakkuk approached Jehovah with a take-no-prisoners fire, and God served it right back. "Watch," said the Lord, "I'm going to do something you won't believe. The Babylonians will wipe out Judah." That explanation didn't settle with the prophet. Why would God use this enemy, the wickedest nation of all, to slaughter his people? Judah appeared righteous compared to it! He asked God about this, too.

The Lord replied that he controls the world, despite its wickedness, and his purposes will prevail. After the Babylonian army defeats the Jews, God will destroy the marauding pagans, too. "I haven't overlooked their evil. I will punish it," he explained. "But my plans differ from yours because you can't view the whole picture. I am the Lord, Habakkuk, and you aren't."

Humbled and put in his place, Habakkuk asked God to "in [his] wrath remember mercy" (Habakkuk 3:2) for those who still worshiped him. Then like the tortured Job, the prophet responded with one of the Scripture's greatest expressions of faith:

> I heard and my heart pounded,
>> my lips quivered at the sound;
> decay crept into my bones,
>> and my legs trembled.
> Yet I will wait patiently for the day of calamity
>> to come on the nation invading us.
> Though the fig tree does not bud
>> and there are no grapes on the vines,
> though the olive crop fails
>> and the fields produce no food,
> though there are no sheep in the pen
>> and no cattle in the stalls,
> yet I will rejoice in the LORD,
>> I will be joyful in God my Savior. (verses 16-18)

Though terrified, Habakkuk vowed to trust and celebrate the Lord in the coming destitution. The prophet acquiesced that only God ruled the world; only the Lord could be an earthling's strength and safety.

Bible teachers use Habakkuk's story to illustrate God's sovereignty and faithfulness, despite the circumstances. But the prophet's dialogue also encourages me to express frustrations to God. The Creator may reply with straightforward and startling answers, but he patiently handles the questions, the anger, the narrow viewpoints of his children. He doesn't punish us for outbursts. He remembers our origins in dust and acts accordingly. He's expansive and merciful enough to handle our brays and foot stomping.

Especially through hardship, we can vent candidly to God. If anything, this clears the soul, shielding it from bitterness, but it also develops an authentic relationship with him. (Sometimes, when we'd rather bail out than keep the faith, yelling is the *only* thing that sustains our communication with him.) Honest wrestling can transport us from unbelief to faith, from protectiveness to vulnerability, from resistance and rebellion to acceptance and surrender. In contrast, masking our gnarled feelings eventually stiffens us, and God doesn't want wooden followers. He purposes to mold soft and pliable hearts, and the sensitivity bares us to raw emotions, both positive and negative, which need expression.

As with Abraham, Sarah, Moses, Naomi, Jeremiah, Peter, Paul, and others, the Lord hears our range of feelings, the emotions he created, and still honors us. I don't recall any of those biblical people pasting a smile on their faces and just saying, "Well, praise the Lord!" They complained and squirmed, doubted and dared God to prove himself. (Even the Virgin Mary asked questions before surrendering to God's mission for her.) Only after they wrestled with God could they accept his words and trust him, and sometimes they didn't completely believe until the Lord fulfilled his promises, despite their skepticism.

Why do we think we're sinning if we express negative feelings? Shaming believers for their emotions and humanness doesn't fit the biblical model. (Yes, habitual complaining earned God's rebuke, but not the questioning that moved people forward in their faith.) Instead, an honest venting brought strugglers closer to God, enabling them to accept his sovereignty and release their frustration. We honor God by rendering our hearts to him.

---

*Trust in him at all times, O people;*
*pour out your hearts to him,*
*for God is our refuge.*

—PSALM 62:8

# Holy Wrestling

*Frederick Buechner*

Out of the deep night a stranger leaps. He hurls himself at Jacob, and they fall to the ground, their bodies lashing through the darkness. It is terrible enough not to see the attacker's face, and his strength is more terrible still, the strength of more than a man. All the night through they struggle in silence until just before morning when it looks as though a miracle might happen. Jacob is winning. The stranger cries out to be set free before the sun rises. Then, suddenly, all is reversed.

He merely touches the hollow of Jacob's thigh, and in a moment Jacob is lying there crippled and helpless. The sense we have, which Jacob must have had, is that the whole battle was from the beginning fated to end this way, that the stranger had simply held back until now, letting Jacob exert all his strength and almost win so that when he was defeated, he would know that he was truly defeated; so that he would know that not all the shrewdness, will, and brute force that he could muster were enough to get this. Jacob will not release his grip, only now it is not of violence but of need, like the grip of a drowning man.

The darkness has faded just enough so that for the first time he can dimly see his opponent's face. And what he sees is something more terrible than the face of death—the face of love. It is vast and strong, half ruined with suffering and fierce with joy, the face a man flees all the darkness of his days until at last he cries out, "I will not let you go until you bless me!" Not a blessing that he can have now by the strength of his cunning or the force of his will, but a blessing that he can have only as a gift.

Power, success, happiness, as the world knows them, are his who will fight for them hard enough; but peace, love, joy, are only from God. And God is the enemy whom Jacob fought there by the river, of course, and whom in one way or another we all of us fight—God, the beloved enemy. Our enemy because, before giving us everything, before giving us life, he demands our lives—our selves, our wills, our treasure.

Will we give them, you and I?

*— The Magnificent Defeat, 1966*

# Naked I Come

*How calmly we may commit ourselves*
*to the hands of him who bears up the world.*
—JEAN PAUL RICHTER

Talk to men and women who've stayed in a hospital, and they'll describe the humiliations thereof. First, there's the hospital gown, making us aware of our backsides as never before. I think those gowns are a medical conspiracy to keep patients in bed. Who wants to roam the halls— or even cross the room—and be exposed? But just when we've grown accustomed to the breeze, the situation gets worse. We regress to wearing a sheet. At this stage—whether for routine checkups or specific tests or scheduled surgery—there's all manner of personal exposure while doctors prod us. And no matter how we try to divert them, they'll eventually pull back the cover and say hello.

I learned this the hard way. In an emotional whirlwind I checked into the hospital only hours after a dermatologist discovered malignant melanoma spreading on my upper right arm. The surgeon scheduled me for his knife that next morning. In the meantime, a parade of doctors and interns visited me to examine the cancerous and now infamous mole, taking photos of it and stepping out of my hearing range to talk. "Wish I'd been this popular in high school," I quipped, trying to stay calm and feeling relieved when they left.

Later that evening my surgeon's intern assistant surprised me with a visit. "I'm here to see the mole on your shoulder," he announced. I didn't like his haughty bedside manner, but I pulled out my arm for display. He scrutinized it. "I understand you also have a small mole to be removed from under your breast," he said.

I did. That mole wasn't malignant, but the surgeon wanted to remove it as a precaution. *But there's no way I'll show it to you,* I thought. My surgeon, a fatherly type, hovered around age sixty. The intern looked about my age—in his early twenties—and far from paternal. "Yes, I do have a mole there," I replied and crossed my arms over my chest. He understood the unsubtle message and said nothing more about it.

I congratulated myself for keeping my private parts private. But the next morning as I rolled into surgery, I suddenly realized that to remove the precautionary mole, a team of mostly strangers would strip me to the waist. *I've spent my life covering up, and in a few moments these guys will expose me in one swoop,* I thought as the anesthesia seeped in. *Years of modesty destroyed.* As I drifted toward sleep, the last face I remember was the surgeon's assistant, waiting to pull back the sheet.

■　　■　　▩

Nakedness elicits emotional responses—not just our own nudity, but the skin baring of others, too. Usually the setting determines how we respond. A baby toddling and dripping and giggling across the living room after a bath spreads a smile across his mother's face. The same child in a pornographer's studio horrifies not just the parents, but society in general. Disrobing before a trusted spouse evokes bliss; undressing for a doctor feels uncomfortable, but manageable if it's kept clinical; peeling off clothes for a rapist is unbearable. A razor sharp line separates the pure from the profane, the delightful from the disgusting. What God intends for good, if not valued and protected, might be tattered and tormented by evil.

The movie *Schindler's List* uncovers a hideous abuse of nudity when the Nazis force Jewish concentration camp prisoners to strip and jog in a wide circle before German officers and doctors. Leering and jeering, the Nazis determine which prisoners appear healthy and still able to work and which look aged or sickly and useless for labor. Then the self-appointed judges doom the unhealthy victims to death by oven, gas chamber, or firing squad. As I watched this atrocity, based on actual events, I sickened. What if this were my mother, my father? The thought of my mom, modest and always careful to cover herself, parading nude before wicked strangers, wouldn't penetrate my brain. It was too unconscionable, yet I couldn't deny that sons and daughters had actually witnessed this humiliation.

Such nudity blasphemes God, perverting the beauty of his creation. In the beginning the first man and woman lived naked and unashamed. Adam and Eve didn't need clothes until they sinned and the nudity embarrassed them. Before evil intruded, the couple felt safe with God and each other. Physically, we may recover vestiges of this security within a few structures, but never universally, on the earth. Sin permanently altered our vision. However, we can still find safety in spiritual nakedness. The Lord doesn't shame a soul laid bare before him.

In fact, God requires spiritual nudity if we're to obtain his assistance, heal our wounds, and extricate ourselves from a pit. This means fully and repeatedly confessing our sins and honestly recounting what ails us—an exposure our pride abhors. Neville Aysgarth, the protagonist in the novel *Ultimate Prizes* by Susan Howatch, represents the everyman who refuses to face his pain until it's almost too late. Neville serves as archdeacon in the Church of England and resolutely polishes his exterior into the perfectly behaved clergyman. Then he marries a young socialite who throws him into drinking, obsession, hypocrisy, and other forms of unhappiness. As Neville encounters each new misery, he admits to "ringing down the curtain" on his feelings and shoving ahead in denial, except the drapery threatens to rise without his consent after he piles too much behind it. On the brink of ruin, the staunch

Englishman who hates emotional nakedness must admit the truth or lose everything.

That's also true for us. Not until we lift the curtain and expose our sin and pain, can we start recovery. This full disclosure benefits us more than God because he already knows everything. However, "confession is good for the soul" because it marks that we're forgiven and secure in God's hands. When we say to him, "Naked, I come, Lord," we're safe, as God always intended. We step from behind the curtain onto holy ground.

---

*Nothing in all creation is hidden from God's sight.*
*Everything is uncovered and laid bare before the eyes*
*of him to whom we must give account.*

—HEBREWS 4:13

# The Only Choice

*The last of the human freedoms*
*is to choose one's attitudes.*
— VIKTOR FRANKL

I watched numbly as a mover tilted my expensive sofa, tightly wrapped in plastic, and shoved it against a wall in the storage unit. I'd thoughtfully chosen that couch, arranged for special fabric and hand construction, and paid cash for it on layaway with budget-stretching installments. Now it stood, upended, next to my cherrywood entertainment center, purchased in the same careful manner, and stacks of boxed-up art books and biographies. I adored those books, purchased through the years at art museums and bookstores around the country when I traveled for business. They belonged to a couple thousand titles in my library, all of which mattered to me. *Everything* in this oversized garage—all of my belongings—mattered to me, and I couldn't predict how long they'd be closed in or whether they'd be pulled out in decent shape, given the rain and snow in Colorado.

I'd heard stories about friends losing their homes through financial downturns, but I never dreamed it'd happen to me. Even when they extolled the peculiar freedom of abandoning encumbrances, I'd prayed silently, *Lord, thank you that I don't have that much freedom.* A home symbolized security to me, even if I merely rented it, and a beautifully decorated house meant even more. Where I lived represented my tastes, values, interests, and creativity—my uniqueness. Living alone, I could be thoroughly myself, an identity sometimes robbed in the workplace, family relationships, and a few friendships, so I carefully guarded my independence. Home was my nest, my safety net, my identity. Home was me.

Home was also slipping away. When I initially rented the house, my landlord planned on selling it "in a year or two." However, she kept stalling, and I continued leasing because I favored the late nineteenth century charm and wanted to own it. Several years later when she finally decided to unhand the house, by then colorfully wallpapered and furnished by me, my income had crashed. I couldn't afford the mortgage.

This collision in timing, though distressing enough on its own, pointed to a bigger crisis than home ownership. Would I continue to follow God's call to write? Answering yes demanded scaling down my lifestyle—way down. With my tottering health I couldn't work a full-time job and still muster the energy to create, and so far I couldn't find steady part-time work to supplement the writing. Accepting a full-time job assured a predictable paycheck, but neglected my calling. Viewed from that perspective, it wasn't much of a decision. From past blunders I'd learned that saying no to God guaranteed misery. Downward mobility felt deeply disappointing, but spiritually it composed the only feasible solution, the only choice.

I decided to sell the flowers in my gardens, store most of my possessions, and rent a small apartment for about six months until my income increased. But that plan turned problematic: either the rent was too high, the lease too long, or my cats too many. Earlier my friend Mary had suggested that I move in with her, but my pride wouldn't consider it and I mentally compiled my reasons. First, I wanted to keep my independence, my way of keeping a home so I wouldn't lose my identity. Second, Mary and I were thorough opposites. Our opinions, food choices, work schedules, leisure activities, housekeeping habits, reading materials—just about everything from all dimensions—dramatically differed. We enjoyed our go-to-the-movies friendship, but sharing a house? I envisioned the rising smoke. Third, to me Mary's décor looked like early Salvation Army (style isn't a priority for her), and fourth, she already owned two cats. Neither were declawed (they'd scratch my furniture) or wanted additional roommates (they'd attack the boys). And two single women living together with four cats? The stereotype unnerved me.

■   ■   ■

Bothered by the potential roommate conflicts, I zigzagged around town in between writing deadlines, searching for the ideal place to land with Monet and Wolfie in tow. I didn't succeed, and two days before my lease terminated, I pursued my only choice. I called Mary and tried to say cheerily, "Hi, roommate." With amazing patience she welcomed me and two distressed cats into her home, after toiling until early morning helping me clean my place. Finally at Mary's house, I pushed a couple pieces of my furniture into a small bedroom and slept on a blow-up mattress on the aging carpet, with freaked-out cats crying through the night. The room had no bed, no curtains, no ambiance. Behind the closed door I cried too.

I'd like to say that following God's will and divesting my stuff filled me with unspeakable joy, but the only unmentionable emotion was sorrow. Grateful for an affordable place to live, I bolstered up at the house and grieved privately at the cheaply priced office I'd rented for business. "Judy, when God wants to use somebody, he prunes her back to the roots," my mother suggested, extending sympathy. "Mom, I'm cut to the nubs," I sighed. God had stabbed and uprooted a materialistic icon sunk in my soul, and it hurt. My "chosen" status, void of beauty and privacy, didn't placate me. I needed time to adjust.

Contrary to my plan, I've lived at Mary's house for three years, and won't be moving out anytime soon. I still miss my home, still feel the loss, and pray for a house of my own, but God has changed and surprised me through avenues I didn't think possible. Because of our pronounced differences, not in spite of them. We can irritate one another, but mostly Mary and I get along well, with humor and respect, and I appreciate the mutual caring about jobs, health, schedules, and families. (We seldom try changing each other; it's tiring and futile.) The cats formed a pecking order, fighting less as the months passed, with Monet and Wolfie feeling comfortably at home. During my low- or no-income months, Mary has shared food, money, and other resources with us. I can't imagine how I'd have survived otherwise. At last, I'm understanding that what's in the heart matters more than what's in the house.

Sometimes the only choice is the best choice because it's God's choice.

---

*You did not choose me, but I chose you and appointed you*
*to go and bear fruit—fruit that will last. Then the Father*
*will give you whatever you ask in my name.*

—JOHN 15:16

# Leaning into the Pain

*Facing the darkness, admitting the pain,*
*allowing the pain to be pain, is never easy.*
*That is why courage—big heartedness—*
*is the most essential virtue on the spiritual journey.*
—MATTHEW FOX

I opened my eyes and stared at the wall, my nose squashed against its yellow paint. Sometime in the night my cat Wolfie had commandeered the bed and sprawled across the sheets, mercilessly relegating me to a corner where I supposedly belonged. *Kind of like my life,* I thought. *Pushed up against the wall.*

I rolled over and Wolfie leapt from the mattress to avoid getting smashed in return. He meowed and I sighed. Neither of us wanted morning to arrive: It signaled surrender. He needed to abandon his privileged spot and I had to admit that pain still spread through my body like an infusion of hot liquid. I pushed up, groped across the room to uncap a bottle on the dresser and swallowed a pain pill.

"No breakfast yet, guys," I told the cats looking up at me expectantly. I crawled back into bed and unleashed tears. *Please, God, just let me go back to sleep.*

In the last year my body had metamorphosed into an unpredictable network of raw nerve endings and stiff muscles and nothing I tried naturally or medically spelled relief except pain medication. Massages, hot and cold packs, and other manipulations only partially helped for a few hours. Medical tests appeared normal, and so far I had no diagnosis. I also suffered with migraines, chronic fatigue, and other symptoms

I'd rather not describe in print. Meeting me outside of the house, most people couldn't tell I didn't feel well, but I could keep up the charade only a few hours and then grabbed pain pills and a long nap. Some days I dropped to my office floor and slept; other times I drove home and conked out until evening. Sometimes I never reached the office at all, though deadlines encroached and editors pressed me for manuscripts.

For a couple of decades, I'd fashioned myself as a professional superwoman, capable of large amounts of work if I just persisted. Now it required unclaimable energy to read my e-mail. For fear of losing projects, I didn't want hardly anyone to know, but that only exacerbated the situation. People waiting for my work didn't understand the slow-down and understandably grew frustrated or markedly angry with me. When I finally admitted the problem, I could only describe it nebu-lously because I didn't have a name for it. Folks understand cancer or arthritis, but without a label I risked sounding more mentally than physically plagued. That only made me feel worse. I was tired of feeling horrible, tired of trying to explain, tired of wondering if I'd steered emo-tionally off course.

Then one day I decided to stop fighting it. I don't know why I sud-denly thought this; maybe the prayers of friends and family finally seeped in. I accepted that I couldn't breeze through a week like other people, that for now I needed more rest than most of them, and I might never regain the energy I once thoughtlessly enjoyed. But that was okay with me, and I started redefining myself. I could still work; I just had to quit second guessing what people thought and sort my days differently from theirs. I struggled with constant pain, but I could still cherish life. Many people lived with much worse conditions, and I could appreci-ate my mobility. I could still do most of what I desired, just not with the overdoses of adrenaline I used to demand. And I could cut out the self-pity.

Essentially, I gave myself permission to lean into the pain, cooperating with its rhythms rather than wishing it didn't exist. I still took my medication, but I quit resenting the pain's intrusion in my life and yielded to what God had allowed for now. Somehow that helped me to rest better, to more hopefully pray for healing, to like myself again. By mentally surrendering, I cooperated with what my physical self needed and I emotionally improved. Friends adjusted to my unorthodox sleeping schedule, and when I worked, I didn't berate myself for not lasting longer than a few hours. That loosened my brain and the writing flowed easier.

A comment from my friend Laurel also liberated me. A former Southern belle, she naps in the afternoon and never apologizes for it. "I sleep for a couple of hours and my kids accept it," she said. With that, I started falling into bed with the sun shining but without guilt, comforted that somebody else commits to daylight snoozing. The rest eases my pain and then I work into the evening.

I don't know how to explain it precisely, but sometimes embracing our pain—relinquishing our rage against it—can help us start healing. That's especially true with emotional turmoil. When we're knotted up, God asks us to rest in him. Practical reasons exist for inwardly ceasing to strive and trusting that he's in charge (Psalm 46:10). We probably save ourselves from compounded illnesses and the verge of insanity, and we allow God to operate. We also grow more sensitive toward others who suffer, and like our Lord, we empathize and bear one another's burdens.

During a bone adjustment, my chiropractor said, "When I work with people I carry an image of them whole and healthy until they create that picture themselves." I think that's what God does while we reckon with our physical and emotional pain. He suffers with us and by his wounds we are healed (Isaiah 53:5).

---

*I am the LORD, who heals you.*

—EXODUS 15:26

# The Grace of Surrender

## *Debra Evans*

Come to Me."

When the circumstances of life are beyond our ability to bear them, when there seems to be no way for things to work out, when the rapids hit and the boat threatens to capsize at any moment, when a sudden change in life plans cancels our dreams and reroutes the future, Jesus stands before us, and with His arms open wide, extends this incredible invitation. Surrendering our burdens at His feet and placing each heavy parcel before the cross, we can choose to close our ears to competing commands and confusing directions, and listen for God's voice alone.

Jesus said, "Come to me, all you who are weary and burdened, and I will give you rest. Take my yoke upon you and learn from me, for I am gentle and humble in heart, and you will find rest for your souls. For my yoke is easy and my burden is light" (Matthew 11:28-30). How could Mary have found her burden light on the way to Bethlehem, riding over bumpy roads on the back of a lumbering donkey? [Her story] prompts us to remember that God's graces appear in the midst of a consecrated life as it is actually lived, not in some far-off realm set apart from real human emotional experience.

Surrender never discounts or denies the reality of suffering. When Jesus agonizingly prayed in the Garden of Gethsemane, "Father, if you are willing, take this cup from me; yet not my will, but yours be done" (Luke 22:42), there can be no doubt He knew what was at stake in the battle looming ahead. Quietly facing His accusers, He submitted to their authority, fully recognizing the costs involved. He understood what the terms of His surrender would be.

But that is not all: By laying down His life before His enemies, in obedience to God's will, Jesus demolished the opposition.

Through surrender—bowing before God's mighty throne, laying each struggle before our Father in heaven, casting out all grief and heartache, giving up to Jesus every source of suffering and sin—we participate, with Christ, in His kingdom's victories. We cannot do it on our own. Heeding the Lord's command to surrender, we are continually surprised to find that, somehow, in a way that is totally beyond our comprehension, *He triumphs through us.*

Take heart, then. Pray for the grace of surrender. Receive all the peace and love Jesus freely offers. He is waiting. His arms are open. What He has done for the greatest saints, He surely can do for you and me.

*— Women of Character, 1996*

# Grant Me a Willing Spirit

## *A Prayer for the Wounded*

Create in me a pure heart, O God,
and renew a steadfast spirit within me.
Do not cast me from your presence
or take your Holy Spirit from me.
Restore to me the joy of your salvation
and grant me a willing spirit, to sustain me.

Then I will teach transgressors your ways,
and sinners will turn back to you.
Save me from bloodguilt, O God,
the God who saves me,
and my tongue will sing of your righteousness....
You do not delight in sacrifice, or I would bring it;
you do not take pleasure in burnt offerings.
The sacrifices of God are a broken spirit;
a broken and contrite heart,
O God, you will not despise.

—PSALM 51:10-14,16-17

# PART FOUR

# Necessary Losses

Spiritually, to lose our lives is to gain them. To clutch our lives is to lose them. During times of brokenness we realize that our ways, our plans and desires, aren't working. We tire of the struggle and eventually surrender our expectations to God.

When we hand our lives back to God, he pours his desires into our hearts to accomplish his work, his way. We experience necessary losses, but they're not losses to fear. Surrender opens the door to a deeper walk with God and his unexpected surprises and blessings.

# Losing Control

*The only way we can brush*
*against the hem of the Lord…*
*is to have the courage, the faith,*
*to abandon control.*

—MADELEINE L'ENGLE

My first "official" leadership position parlayed into a conflict I'll never forget. At about age sixteen, I wrote and directed a play produced by my church's youth group. Consequently, on the Saturday before a Sunday evening performance to our small congregation, the thespian-type teenagers among us met at church for an overdue rehearsal.

Despite our eleventh-hour gathering, the potentially stressful rehearsal progressed smoothly—until I decided the play would fare better if we performed in the basement instead of the sanctuary. (I've forgotten the reason I considered this a clever idea.) Not many agreed, but as their leader I thought this meant we did things my way, so cast members begrudgingly hauled our homespun props downstairs, including a couch that barely passed through a narrow stairwell.

Within minutes after hoisting everything downstairs, I figured the basement wasn't the right place after all. *Okay, let's move things back upstairs,* I decided. It made sense to me (I've always needed to see a furniture arrangement before I settle on it), but articulating my decision instigated mutiny. The guys felt especially annoyed because they'd hauled the heavy pieces. I prefer to think I prepared those young men for marriage, but even today they probably wouldn't appreciate the humor.

The final blow occurred when halfway up the stairs the couch got stuck on the railings. We lost our patience, exchanged blaming words, and my last remembrance regarding this production is of me standing on one side of the lodged couch with an angry male on the other, glowering at each other.

In high school I was already a bona fide control freak, at least during church gatherings, but I wouldn't even begrudgingly identify this trait as a weakness. I just thought the noncompliant types weren't very smart or creative, or acted rebellious in groups. Otherwise, why wouldn't they cooperate with ideas as good as mine?

This desire to orchestrate events and people raged much earlier than during my teen years. I remember neighborhood playtimes splintering because of a power struggle over who'd lead the group, or play the "best" role in our make-believe sagas. My friend Peggy and I rivaled over who'd be the club leader, game captain, or play the role of princess in our imaginary castle, which doubled as the wraparound porch at Becky's house. A phlegmatic and a tomboy, Becky didn't care who did what, as long as we could wield a few homemade swords and prove ourselves worthy in the mythical kingdom. But if I couldn't be the It Girl that day, I'd march home crying and complaining to my mother, who'd heard it all before. If Peggy couldn't preside, then she'd leave in a huff. Usually when we schemed up this type of organized play, we hardly got anything done. Somebody would get offended, fracture the project, and stomp home. (I think that's how Becky learned to play happily by herself, which pleased her mom because that created less of a mess.) All this, and we were only in the middle years of grade school.

Unfortunately, I carried this need to control into the workplace, and yet sometimes it actually benefited me. Working by myself, I could pull off lots of projects, nicely done. But interacting with or managing groups, I sometimes stepped on the toes of unsuspecting and not-so-unsuspecting people. Combined with perfectionism, my control mode created a certain way to do everything, and few measured up. In addition, I mistakenly believed that in a well-functioning group or relationship all members travel the same wavelength of thought and action. I wasted time manipulating team members to think like me and do what I felt best for them. Through the years it took conflict and a couple of staff resignations to wake me up to what the team already knew. Though gifted with leadership abilities, I could use them to control people—even my friends—and that produced dissension.

■     ■     ■

In the Old Testament, Laban, the wealthy sheep breeder, fit the description of a controller who mishandled his family. He profited from his sister Rebekah's marriage to Isaac and used his daughters, Rachel and Leah, as bargaining chips to trick his son-in-law Jacob and benefit financially. (See Genesis 24:1–31:55.) Over time Jacob outwitted his father-in-law, but Laban still couldn't admit his wrongdoing and fought for control by requesting that his son-in-law leave Haran. The upshot is that God's will prevailed, despite the shrewdness of a selfish father.

In fact, God will always prevail, and thankfully, it's his desire that we abandon our need to control not just other people but everything about our lives. He's the one who controls outcomes. He wants to direct our paths. As long as we're makeshifting coups of our own, we'll miss his best for us, both in character and direction. I wasted relationships not realizing this, and probably for the rest of my life, I'll need to remind myself to trust God's control instead of my abilities, knowledge, or preparation.

But at least now I can claim I'm a *recovering* control freak. In recent years God has allowed me no control over my career, finances, or future. No slack whatsoever. This has whacked away at my misguided belief that if I just worked hard enough or talked convincingly enough, I'd keep my life the way I wanted it. Somewhere along the way, out of pain and frustration, I loosened my grip. This feels better. Control is consuming, exhausting, disappointing work.

Ultimately as we navigate pain and difficulty, God wants us to hand the control to him. This is harder than it sounds, because once we surrender to the Lord's overall direction, we can still try manipulating the day-by-day details or bending his will to our preference. As I think about that now, it sounds humorously pathetic. Little humans trying to outsmart the immeasurable God. We're ridiculously self-involved, and God will keep "upping the ante" until we can't control our fate anymore and choose to rely on him.

If that sounds selfish of God, here's the good part. He's enormously wiser, kinder, and more generous than we are. He leads us in paths of righteousness for his name's sake (Psalm 23:3) and fulfills our heart's desires (Psalm 145:19). If we pursue those desires our way, eventually we'll misfire, but if we trust and allow him to lead, most likely he'll delight us with the outcome (Psalm 37:4). But first we pass through the valley of the shadow of death, the death of our wily and obstreperous selves. As Christians, if we've lost control, we're probably on the right track.

---

*The LORD has established his throne in heaven,*
*and his kingdom rules over all.*

—PSALM 103:19

# Uncluttering Our Plans

*Do not pretend. Do not lie.*
*Look your struggle in the eye,*
*whenever you can, with help if you need it.*
*And slowly—as slowly as necessary—*
*come to terms with it.*

—DAVID B. BIEBEL

After snags syncing schedules, I finally arranged a dinner with my friends Steve and Annie. We planned it as an adults-only evening at my home so we could relax and talk in depth without kids underfoot. (I scheduled this interlude before I moved out of my house.) Wanting the evening to be an oasis from their stressful lives, I set the table with china and crystal, silver and linens, flowers and candles. And I spent the afternoon trying new recipes for a salad, stuffed pasta shells, and other palette pleasers.

Preparations clipped along smoothly, but then the phone rang. It was Annie. "Bad news," she said. "Our out-of-town guests left awhile ago, only to call from the Interstate to say their car broke down. Steve left in our van to get them, and they'll need to stay at our house again tonight because the weather's getting bad. I guess we can't come over for dinner…"

As she talked, I glanced out the window at unwanted snow flurries. *Oh, no,* I groaned inside, *a lovely night ruined. And I have so much food!* Per usual I'd prepared more meal than needed so I could send guests home with leftovers. But then it hit me: If they couldn't come for dinner, why couldn't dinner go to them? So Annie set a table for nine at her home, I schlepped my entrees across town, and we enjoyed a memorable evening, noisy kids and all. It was *really fun.* Driving home later, the snow had quit falling, as if nature had given up on keeping us apart.

That night taught me volumes about flexibility and the dividends of altering goals that don't match new and unexpected circumstances. It's a simple example, though, compared to what's required when calamity crashes in on us. Something like a sudden death, a job loss, a life-threatening illness, a child with an eating disorder or a drug addiction, a marriage that's about to shatter, a personal moral struggle. The vestiges of a Puritan work ethic may urge us to trudge forward with our usual plans, to keep a sense of normalcy, and that can work for a while. But eventually we wear out and intensify the anxiety or possibly neglect the problem. If we're participants in an ongoing crisis, it's healthful to survey our schedules and unclutter the commitments. If we're going to change or resolve or adjust to the difficulty, it commands focus and time.

We may chafe at this action at first because frequently we define ourselves by what we do. Plus, others depend on us and may not understand why we're pulling out. Of course, it's probably unfeasible to quit a job and definitely unthinkable to stop feeding the family or providing basic necessities. But we can trim back what's not absolutely essential, if it means saving a life or the situation or our sanity. Or even if it simply means learning what God wants to teach us. Altering our plans to accommodate the pressing circumstances, or simply allowing time for restful idleness, can yield great benefits.

Usually we can consider the adjustments or pulling out as temporary—a time to at least reconnect our heads and hearts—if we can't remedy the problem. We can also draw nigh to God, and look back at these days with gratitude, counting our blessings for what we gained, rather than recounting what we lost. I have a friend who shut down her involvements in order to nurse a sick spouse. I heard about an author who quit writing for a year to shore up character flaws. Another friend focused closely on meeting the needs of a prodigal daughter. Still another slowed down to strengthen her spiritual life midst a truckload of disappointments. All would say they felt relieved and benefited after scaling back. Besides, once they ended their time-out, plenty of activities still beckoned for attention. That is, if they wanted to be busy again. When I uncluttered my involvements, working through loss and health problems, I misplaced the desire to crowd my schedule again. I value the more reasonable pace and how much better I feel and act without so many demands dumped on me. Others have experienced the same feelings, especially if busyness caused the difficulty in the first place.

There's no rule about when and how long to pull back, or whether we're to adjust our schedules at all. If we'll do whatever it takes to infiltrate God's will and character into our souls, he'll unfold the rest.

---

*Come to me, all you who are weary and burdened,*
*and I will give you rest.*

—Matthew 11:28

# A Terrifying Opportunity

## M. Craig Barnes

To be born again is to discover ourselves as infants in the gracious arms of God. There is nothing we can do to make God love us more. There is nothing we can do to make him love us less. We cannot manipulate God. He won't pay attention to us if we figure out how to become his favorite child. We assume God's love must be tied to something—our performance, our sacrifices, or at least our love for him. But Scripture is rather clear about this. God's love for us is rooted in his own merciful nature.

Becoming convinced of that grace is like—well, like being born again. We understand that even if we lost the world, the love of the Father would still be enough.

One of the things we have to turn away from is our expectation of glory. Most of us want just a little bit of glory that will put a shine on lives that have been dulled by the harsh realities of limitations and losses. A teacher knocks herself out in hopes that she will make a real difference in one or two students every year. She would love to be recognized as the miracle worker, but she settles for an occasional thank-you note at graduation. A young employee regularly puts in overtime at the office in hopes that the CEO will walk by his desk long after everyone has gone home. It is only a little glory, but we work very hard for it.

Usually our understanding of glory is that it comes as a momentary reward. When God brings glory into our life, though, it comes not as an achievement but as an interruption, not as a moment of recognition but as a terrifying answer to prayer.

Some of us spend most of our lives praying that God will answer a specific prayer. After a while, we get so used to living without the thing we crave that the craving itself turns into our constant companion. Imagine what would happen if God actually gave us the desire of our hearts. We would have to abandon the craving that has become so much a part of life. That would be frightening....

It is striking how much fear the angels created when they announced the births of John the Baptist and Jesus. Zechariah, Mary, Joseph and the shepherds—they all responded in fear to the angelic announcement. That was probably the right response. Whenever God sends a messenger with good news for us, it usually means a complete abandonment of the life into which we have settled.

Mary did not expect to be visited by an angel. We are told that she was perplexed by his arrival, and that she pondered the meaning of his salutation, "Greetings, favored one!" (Luke 1:28, NASB [sic]). When Zechariah saw Gabriel, he was terrified because he knew this was the answer from God for which he had prayed throughout his whole life. But Mary wasn't a priest. She was just a young woman who was certain that if she was going to have a moment of glory in her life, it would be at her coming wedding. Like most Jews in her day, Mary had also come to terms with the reality of how it is. She knew that joy is found in gathering the few good moments that happen in the ordinary routines of life. So she "pondered" the "perplexing" words she heard about God's favor.

■　　　■　　　■

To ponder. To be perplexed. Those are great words. They signal the beginning of a mysterious intrusion. Something is out of the ordinary. A stranger knocks on the door and delivers a cable marked urgent. The boss steps into the office, shuts the door and says, "I need to talk to you." A woman wakes up one morning feeling a little nauseated. They ponder. They get perplexed. The thin veneer of the ordinary has been scratched. They suspect that it's going to cost them plenty.

A favor from God is usually confusing. But that is just how it begins. "Do not be afraid, Mary; for you have found favor with God. And behold, you will conceive in your womb, and bear a son, and you shall name Him Jesus" (Luke 1:30-31, NASB). Then Mary says, "How can this be?" She is no longer perplexed. Now she is terrified. That is a common dynamic in conversion. Once we realize what God is up to, we move from confusion to terror.

This is how God offers a favor? A woman has one great hope for a fleeting moment of glory at her modest wedding to the carpenter down the street. She hears that she has been chosen to give birth to the Messiah. Does she immediately rejoice and say, "Yes! The other women will shun me and spread rumors about me. Joseph will probably refuse to marry me. In fact, according to the law of Moses, I could get stoned for this. But if God wants me to abandon everything I had dreamed of in order to bring hope to the world, I'll just consider myself blessed."

No, Mary didn't ask for God to grant her a favor. She had played by the rules and was still a virgin. By rights she should have been allowed to pursue ordinary dreams. But what we have coming to us by rights is exactly what God overlooks when he decides to give us his favor, his grace. And for most of us, it is very good news that we don't get what we have coming to us by rights.

Many portraits of Mary show her with a quiet, serene smile. But that is not the picture we have of her in Luke, at least not yet. At this point she has just realized that her life is out of control. How can this be? A life so well constructed has to be abandoned. A job is lost. A move has to be made. Another move. A loved one dies way too soon. These interruptions proclaim that life is not what we had hoped for. It isn't even what we had settled for. God has interrupted our ordinary expectations, as cherished as they were, to conceive something. We can't imagine it. We can't even understand it. All we can do is receive it. Because if God has conceived this thing, then it is holy, and it will save our lives.

—*When God Interrupts, 1996*

# Where Did My Life Go?

*We don't have complete emotions
about the present, only about the past.*

— VIRGINIA WOOLF

When Joan moved from California to Colorado, she anticipated work-ing for a nonprofit organization committed to keeping teenagers off drugs. She sold or stored most of her possessions before the transition and considered this mission worthy of a radical lifestyle change. Previ-ously, she'd earned a hearty income selling fashionable clothes to busi-nesswomen and claims she lived large, like "a pampered poodle" with abundant self-care appointments. In Colorado, she shared a house with the ministry director and his wife and slept on a bunk bed in a joltingly plain room. Still, to stoke her passion she determined to accept a simpler lifestyle and paycheck.

She also called me. Joan had read my book *Designing a Woman's Life,* about finding purpose in life, and asked if we could meet. I usually don't book appointments with strangers, but Joan swung into sales mode and we coffee klatsched a few days later. Raising her voice above the Starbucks clatter, she explained that my book motivated her min-istry pursuit. I remember thinking, *How frightening! She moved across country because of something I wrote.* What if her new venture didn't pan out? It'd be partly my fault.

Weeks later circumstances answered my question. Contrary to the original plan, the ministry couldn't afford to keep Joan on salary. She capsized in a new location with no job, no home, few friends, and not much money. At that time I still lived in my rented house, so Joan moved in with me. We joked that, if readers took my book seriously, their lives might fall apart too. Then they'd line up on my front sidewalk, asking for room and board. "It's your responsibility to take care of us, Judy," she laughed, wanting to lighten up the ordeal. But the piercing disappointment was hardly funny. Sometimes I heard Joan sobbing alone in the guest bedroom.

"Where did my life go?" she asked during despairing moments, and I couldn't answer. Why had God allowed this loss? Joan had been so eager, so earnest. What was he up to? Dashing the dreams of a willing servant seemed *so unfair.* Joan's loss was debunking the last of my formulas about how God operates. Even after losing the magazine, I still hoped if I followed God's path there'd be no more setbacks. (Denial runs deep within me. It flows in my veins.) Even though I wrote a chapter about brokenness, and its necessity in fulfilling a mission, when Joan asked, "Why?" my mind blanked. I groped for encouraging words, but whatever I volunteered rang hollow.

▪      ▪      ▪

Who can know God's mind? I certainly can't, and through our losses both Joan and I decided that only in retrospect—often years later—would we view God's intentions. He may unveil glimpses here and there, but mostly, loss challenges our vision. It's as if a midnight fog settles in; we can't see our former life, nor can we discern the future's dimensions. We can only squint at what's inches ahead, and it's dark and scary. We ache for morning to shine away our mourning.

Most of us fear this darkness, the anxious hours from midnight until dawn, but it needn't paralyze us. Though we feel immobilized outwardly, we can advance inwardly, albeit slowly. For our mental and spiritual health, it's crucial to grieve the life we loved and lost. We miss the past and probably want at least slivers of it back. Even if the former scenario wasn't grand, it's the only reality we've known; it's our comfort zone. But as the psychologists say, we need to "get closure" on the past before effectively inhabiting the future. What do we miss? Why? Are we realistic about what life was like "back then," or because of current pain, do we idealize it? What might we regain? What won't return? Reckoning with the answers clears space for a new era's arrival. But the accounting takes time—plenty of it. If we've clung to a particular existence for decades, it's seldom possible to ungrip it immediately.

After this, we can ask God about attitudinally preparing us for the future, about enlarging the soul for his replacement plans. How can we pry open a rusty, locked heart to contain the future? Would the oil-bearing Holy Spirit please help? This request coincides with asking God to increase our faith to believe that something good lies ahead, and to endure until it materializes. Isaiah 43:18-19 serves as a hopeful litany during this blinding waiting period: "Forget the former things; do not dwell on the past. See, I am doing a new thing! Now it springs up; do you not perceive it? I am making a way in the desert and streams in the wasteland."

In the density, God prods us to scrunch our spiritual eyes until they recognize the faint light of his lamp creeping toward us.

---

*See, the former things have taken place,*
*and new things I declare;*
*before they spring into being*
*I announce them to you.*

—ISAIAH 42:9

# Crossing the Threshold

## *Sue Monk Kidd*

A crisis is a holy summons to cross a threshold. It involves both a leaving behind and a stepping toward, a separation and an opportunity.

The word *crisis* derives from the Greek words *krisis* and *krino*, which mean "a separating." The very root of the word implies that our crises are times of severing from old ways and states of being. We need to ask ourselves what it is we're being asked to separate from. What needs to be left behind?

As I asked myself the question, I drew courage from a Bible story. One man who came to Jesus wanting to be a disciple said, "Let me first go and bury my father." Jesus gave him what seems like a harsh answer: "Follow me, and leave the dead to bury their own dead" (Matthew 8:21-22, RSV). But when you apply the answer to the process of inner transformation, it makes perfect sense. This is a call to separation. To "leave the dead." In order to follow the inner journey, we need to leave behind those things that are deadening, the loyalties that no longer have life for us.

Crisis is a separation, but it's equally a time of opportunity. The Chinese word for *crisis* is composed of two characters. On top is the sign for danger; beneath it is the sign for opportunity. That character graphically illustrates the saying, "Crisis is really another name for redirection."

A minister friend of mine, who has seen countless Christians through crisis events, told me that he didn't think most Christians know *how* to have a crisis—at least not creatively.

He started me wondering. For the most part, we do one of two things in response to a crisis. We say that it's God's will and force ourselves into an outwardly sweet acceptance, remaining unaffected at the deeper level of the spirit. People who have a crisis in this manner are generally looking for comfort and peace of mind.

Or we reject the crisis, fighting and railing against it until we become cynical and defeated or suffer a loss of faith. People who choose this way to have a crisis are after justice.

Yet there's a third way to have a crisis: the way of waiting. That way means creating a painfully honest and contemplative relationship with one's own depths, with God in the deep center of one's soul. People who choose this way aren't so much after peace of mind or justice as wholeness and transformation. They're after soulmaking.

If you choose this way, you find the threshold, the creative moment of epiphany, within the crisis. You discover that the stormy experience can be an agent drawing you deeper into the kingdom, separating you from the old consciousness and the clamp of the ego. It's not an easy way....

Jesus had some curious things to say about the way a person comes into the inner kingdom of the True Self. You do it, he said, by entering a "narrow gate," which only a few folks ever find (Luke 13:24, NKJV). You do it by way of tight, difficult, uncomfortable places that separate you out from the rest of the herd.

In another biblical reference Jesus proclaimed, "I have come to bring fire to the earth" (Luke 12:49, NLT). The coming of the inner kingdom often erupts through a fiery experience. That verse reminds me of the moment in the *Divine Comedy* when Dante enters the searing fire through which all persons must pass in order to make their way to Paradiso, the dwelling of God.

Dante is afraid of the flames; but he's assured that it's okay to enter, for this is the fire that burns but does not consume. To walk through this fire is not to die but to be transformed and purged. That is the fire of Christ.

— *When the Heart Waits*, 1990

# A Good Vision for Sale

*What lies behind us and what lies before us
are small matters compared to
what lies within us.*
—RALPH WALDO EMERSON

After Joan's ministry dream disintegrated, she grabbed the next logical option. My spirited friend discarded the work-with-teens vision and resolved to construct another pastoral goal. Unfortunately, after mailing out capable résumés and scudding around in impeccable suits, nothing panned out, except her dwindled bank account.

Circumstances indicated that Joan wasn't intended for those ministries, either, so she fervently applied for secular jobs as a temporary fix. More paperwork and schmoozing ensued, and Joan restaked familiar territory: sales and marketing. Actually, she yanked up and replanted those stakes several times in the next year or so. One job after another fizzled, usually for reasons beyond Joan's control, and no full-time ministry positions emerged. Just what did God want? Couldn't he see how seriously she was trying? What was she supposed to do now? Accustomed to success, she hadn't groomed a response to failure. Most of us don't, until defeat outdistances us.

Disheartened and rummaging for work, Joan accepted a job as a benefits consultant to labor union workers. "God must have a good sense of humor," she joked, "because I'm completely out of my element." She closeted the upscale wardrobe, gritted her motivation, and drove for hours to visit clients in working-class towns, miles from a desire to minister and love her daily tasks.

At this juncture most of us would pound a sign in the front yard that promises, "A Good Vision for Sale." We're ready to sell, endow, or dump the mission we thought was God-inspired. Perhaps we intercepted the wrong signal, a communication beaming toward someone else. That someone might possess the skill to tame this bucking vision and terminate our anguish. But with this conclusion beware: We could be stomping on life-threatening ground, about to commit a crime against the soul. Sometimes we're to discard a vision because we whipped it up ourselves, but loss and dead ends don't necessarily indicate we fabricated something and should confess. Before redirecting ourselves we need to dwell in this land, to be faithful in the small things, to wait out the dry season. It could be that we received the right vision, but misinterpreted its timing or fulfillment. It could be that God wants to implement his plan but first needs to maneuver us out of the way. It could be that our Lord won't hurry and this tests our patience. Or that he's sharpening our character before we dig in deep. Be careful not to smother a flickering dream just before it bursts into flames.

Loss frequently accompanies those who eventually achieve their dreams; it especially visits God's visionaries. Spiritually, we lose our lives to gain them, but not just our unconverted selves. As believers we bury dreams and projects, often against our will, so God can resurrect his purposes, divine and untainted, in us. And he never relinquishes his ability to astonish.

Joan kept working, still wishing for ministry prospects, and God imaginatively fulfilled her desires. As the benefits job prospered, so did her opportunities to spiritually influence high school and college students. She's mentored one-on-one, taught Bible studies, and traveled with young people for a national gathering and an overseas missions trip. A startling ministry venue erupted after the fatal springtime shootings at Columbine High School in Littleton, Colorado. Joan counseled bereaved students, and a coalition of churches hired her to organize a late-summer concert for that community, in which many teens committed their lives to Christ before starting the new school year. Organizing this event obliged Joan to request a sabbatical and reside in Littleton for six weeks. Because Joan had become one of the company's top consultants in Colorado, her manager, though not a believer, consented with his blessings.

So far Joan's spiritual input to teens and young adults hasn't burgeoned under an organization's umbrella, but most of the involvements required the mobility of a "freelancer" rather than someone obligated to a full-time ministry position. Her secular job provided the income and flexibility she needed. Today Joan still works at the job she doesn't love, but I anticipate more amazing stories ahead and maybe a transition into full-time ministry. Anything's possible because God's vision is sharper than ours. And in the meantime, she's been faithful and he's not wasting her life.

---

*For the vision is yet for an appointed time, but at the end*
*it shall speak, and not lie: though it tarry, wait for it;*
*because it will surely come, it will not tarry.*

—HABAKKUK 2:3, KJV

# Losing Face

*If you've found meaning in your life,*
*you don't want to go back.*
— MORRIE SCHWARTZ

Lately my girlfriends and I are sharing sorrows about our aging faces, worrying about their eventual resemblance to farm animals. One friend frets that the outside corners of her eyes are beginning to look like chicken tracks. Another woman waddles toward the title Turkey Neck; yet another thinks *bullfrog* when she surveys the space below her jaw. I'm sure that in a few years my eyelids will misrepresent me as a drooping donkey. We've joked about gravity's pull, wondering if plastic surgeons offer group rates, but mostly we're trying, reluctantly, to adjust. We're gradually losing our familiar facades without knowing what will replace them and hoping we'll avoid a doctor's knife to preserve our identities.

Actually, our response to all loss—physical, material, spiritual, or otherwise—funnels down to this question: Will we try to save face, or not? Will we rescue our pride and cover up, or just let it all hang? Western culture pushes us to bury the pain, regroup, and act like we're successful. To save our reputation we're to deny, overcome, or kick away loss—whatever positions us in the best possible light, in the winner's circle. Looking our best in spite of the worst is an appealing approach, but it's not what Jesus taught.

Christ introduced his followers to a lifetime of loss. For example, we're to lose our worldly attachment to pride, reputation, materialism, personal will, self-sufficiency, striving to be first, and earthly rewards.

He doesn't promise we'll regain them, either. We're not to revive, restructure, or reinvest in them. They're meant to be permanent losses. We're not to save face, but to live with the loss in plain view.

Even more, Christ blessed the people who lived with loss: the weak, the poor, the sick, the blind, the disabled, the disoriented. He blesses us when we lose too. He offers us the gift of humility, the opportunity to dwell in his grace. From what I've observed about human nature, we don't release worldly attitudes and accept heaven's humility graciously, until we lose something materially important to us, something we thought rightfully belonged to us. An unseen knife severs our attachment, but through the grief we finally recognize the freedom and the relief of releasing self-preservation. We walk in the light as Christ does (1 John 1:7). We don't care what people think any more; there's nothing else to lose. We accept our falling faces as they are.

---

*Your attitude should be the same as that of Christ Jesus:*

*Who, being in very nature God,*
*did not consider equality with God*
*something to be grasped,*
*but made himself nothing.*

—Philippians 2:5-7

# In God I Trust

## *A Prayer for the Fearful*

When I am afraid,
I will trust in you.
In God, whose word I praise,
in God I trust; I will not be afraid.
What can mortal man do to me?

All day long they twist my words;
they are always plotting to harm me....

Record my lament;
list my tears on your scroll—
are they not in your record?

Then my enemies will turn back
when I call for help.
By this I will know that God is for me.
In God, whose word I praise,
in the LORD, whose word I praise—
in God I trust; I will not be afraid.
What can man do to me?

—PSALM 56:3-5,8-11

# Our Daily Dread

*Relying on God has to begin all over again
every day as if nothing had yet been done.*

—C. S. LEWIS

One of the worst aspects of living with loss and disappointment is the dailyness of it. For an extended time we awaken each morning to the unbending fact that nothing's changed. We're still aching, what we cherished probably won't materialize, and sadness gnaws into the soul. Reality bites and leaves a substantial hole. Waking up becomes a daily dread because it feels like losing all over again.

That could be why in the middle of Lamentations, a book of sorrow and complaint, the author assures us of God's grace and presence: "Because of the LORD's great love we are not consumed, for his compassions never fail. They are new every morning; great is your faithfulness. I say to myself, 'The LORD is my portion; therefore I will wait for him.' The LORD is good to those whose hope is in him, to the one who seeks him; it is good to wait quietly for the salvation of the LORD" (Lamentations 3:22-26).

When we dread the day, Scripture reminds us that God will pour his mercy and compassion into our gaping hearts. He greets us each morning with his love. Before lumbering from bed, we can wait a few moments, remind ourselves of his presence, and ask for mercy and compassion once again. We need not fear him growing tired of our unrelenting request because his well of loving-kindness never runs dry; it's designed to replenish us continually. For each daily loss he supplies his endless daily mercy.

If we practice this exchange regardless of our feelings, in the spiritual realm we're substituting his strength for our weakness, filling the inner chasm with his reassurances. Day by day, we replace the loss with God's healing love, until we can claim, "You came near when I called you, and you said, 'Do not fear.' O Lord, you took up my case; you redeemed my life" (verses 57-58). We've lessened the searing pain and increased our awareness of his boundless presence.

---

*Praise be to the Lord, to God our Savior,*
*who daily bears our burdens.*

—PSALM 68:19

# Losing Guilt

*I put it to you that nothing is more important
than that you should make your confession...
at the very earliest opportunity.*

—SUSAN HOWATCH, GLITTERING IMAGES

A friend recently joined the Orthodox Church, and I scrambled to understand how this step departed from our evangelical protestant roots. Was Orthodoxy like being Catholic? or a fundamentalist who recites the liturgy? or a charismatic but with bells-and-smells rituals? I'd mentally cataloged a working knowledge of several branches of Christianity, but couldn't easily wrap my brain around this one. How, exactly, did my friend practice her faith now? And was she out on a limb?

After visiting a vespers service at her church—and discovering I'm allergic to incense—I decided to investigate. But instead of my plying her with questions, she piled me with books and pamphlets, and I read about this curious faith. This arm of Orthodoxy (Antiochian) traces its roots to the church after Christ's ascension, stands on a firm scriptural foundation, centers on salvation through faith, and worships with an ancient liturgy developed by early Christians. It has also revitalized and deepened my friend's devotion to God through the continuity and steadfastness of its traditions. Considering all that, I couldn't fuss about Orthodoxy's core theology or its influence on my friend, although I differ on the peripheral beliefs and don't plan to change my perch on the universal Church's family tree anytime soon.

Still, an intriguing aspect of Orthodox traditions and other ritualistic Christian groups is the emphasis on regular, guided confession. As a

Protestant, I believe we're free to confess sins directly to God at any time, and I wonder if the liturgy, Eucharist, and confessional can evolve into empty ritual without sincere repentance. But placing that question aside, I could value the practice of a formalized time for confession. It gets the job done. In prayer we can grow so absorbed with requests, or even the emotions of praise and thanksgiving, that we minimize or forget confession. Yet the Bible indicates our need to confess sin and receive forgiveness, to build no walls of iniquity between God and us so he hears those prayers (Psalm 66:18).

Stated that way, confession should infiltrate the spiritual life. However, in the everyday tussle it's easy to omit asking for pardon, to postpone confession until "there's enough time" or we've conjured up sorrowful feelings. But often these self-imposed requirements aren't fulfilled until the guilt presses so smolderingly against us, we can't stand the heat anymore. In Psalm 38 David admitted to declining health and a troubled spirit because of his unconfessed sin (verses 3,5,7,18). Proverbs 5:22 warns us that the cords of sin hold us fast. Jesus said everyone who sins is a slave to sin (John 8:34). So for obvious reasons it's better to wash off the offense soon after it occurs: to wade, refresh, and heal in the cool waters of God's forgiveness. A formal practice of confession—someone or something prompting us to repent—could hasten the process.

When we're hurt, grieved, and otherwise stressed or distressed, confession plays a critical, relieving role. Stacking unconfessed sin atop weighty circumstances sinks the soul, either imprisoning us in our tracks or slogging us toward nowhere. We lighten our load with genuine confession and believing—truly accepting—that Christ forgives and releases us from sin's burden, even the guilt of repeated transgressions.

At the soul's core, less becomes more.

---

*If we confess our sins, he is faithful and just and will*
*forgive us our sins and purify us from all unrighteousness.*

—1 JOHN 1:9

# The Bright Darkness

## *Brennan Manning*

When we have hit bottom and are emptied of all we thought important to us, then we truly pray, truly become humble and detached, and live in the bright darkness of faith. In the midst of the emptying we know that God has not deserted us. He has merely removed the obstacles keeping us from a deeper union with him. Actually, we are closer to God than ever before, although we are deprived of the consolations that we once associated with our spirituality. What we thought was communion with him was really a hindrance to that communion.

Yet the dark night is not the end—only the means to union with God. We have asked God for the gift of prayer and he visits us with adversity to bring us to our knees. We have prayed for humility and God levels us with humiliation. We cry out for an increase of faith and God strips us of the reassurances that we have identified with faith. Does growth in Christ follow automatically?

No. Suffering alone does not produce a prayerful spirit. Humiliation alone does not foster humility. Desolation alone does not guarantee the increase of faith. These experiences merely dispose us to prayer, humility, and faith. We can still be wallowing in self-pity and rebellion, pride or apathy, and the last state will be worse than the first. We can eat humble pie until the bakery is bare and emerge with only tight-fisted bitterness in our hands. One further crucial step in the process of ego-slaying remains.

The most characteristic feature of the humility of Jesus is his for-giveness and acceptance of others. By contrast, our nonacceptance and lack of forgiveness keep us in a state of agitation and unrest. Our re-sentments reveal that the signature of Jesus is still not written on our lives. The surest sign of union with the crucified Christ is our forgive-ness of those who have perpetuated injustices against us. Without ac-ceptance and forgiveness the dark night will only be that. The bottom line will be a troubled heart. Forgiveness of enemies seals our participa-tion in the dark night of Jesus Christ who cried out on behalf of his killers: "Forgive them, Father, they know not what they do."

■   ■   ■

Forgiveness is the key to everything. It forms the mind of Christ within us and prevents the costly and painful process of the dark night from itself becoming an ego trip. It guards us from feeling so "spiritually advanced" that we look down on those who are still enjoying the com-forts and consolations of the first conversion. The "gentle and humble in heart" have the mind of Christ.

Henri Nouwen tells the story of an old man who used to meditate early every morning under a big tree on the bank of the Ganges River. One morning, after he had finished his meditation, the old man opened his eyes and saw a scorpion floating helplessly in the water. As the scor-pion was washed closer to the tree, the old man quickly stretched him-self out on one of the long roots that branched out into the river and reached out to rescue the drowning creature. As soon as he touched it, the scorpion stung him. Instinctively, the man withdrew his hand. A minute later, after he had regained his balance, he stretched himself out again on the roots to save the scorpion. This time the scorpion stung him so badly with its poisonous tail that his hand became swollen and bloody and his face contorted with pain.

At that moment, a passerby saw the old man stretched out on the roots struggling with the scorpion and shouted: "Hey, stupid old man, what's wrong with you? Only a fool would risk his life for the sake of an ugly, evil creature. Don't you know you could kill yourself trying to save that ungrateful scorpion?"

The old man turned his head. Looking into the stranger's eyes, he said calmly, "My friend, just because it is the scorpion's nature to sting, that does not change my nature to save."

Sitting here at the typewriter in my study, I turn to the symbol of the crucified Christ on the wall to my left. And I hear Jesus praying for his murderers, "Father, forgive them. They do not know what they are doing."

The scorpion he had tried to save had finally killed him. To me, the passerby, who sees him stretched out on the tree roots and who shouts, "Only a madman would risk his life for the sake of an ugly, ungrateful creature," Jesus answers, "My friend, just because it is fallen mankind's nature to wound, that does not change my nature to save."

Here is the final repudiation of the ego. We surrender the need for vindication, hand over the kingdom of self to the Father, and in the sovereign freedom of forgiving our enemies, celebrate the luminous darkness.

— *The Signature of Jesus*, 1996

# PART FIVE

# Drawing Nearer

In the darkness and discipline of brokenness—when our lives feel at a standstill and certain prayers don't yield perceptible answers—we're inclined to shove God aside and tinker with the problems ourselves. But we also know he's our only hope for something better; we crave his undeserved mercy, forgiveness, and intervention.

Remarkably, without vengefulness, the Lord compassionately responds. He showers grace in our time of need, though we still sit in the shadow. When we accept this grace, we catch glimmers of hope, comfort, and thankfulness. But most of all, when we draw nearer to God, we discover him in new and profound ways.

# The Door

*Difficult circumstances seem to increase*
*our ability to experience intimacy with Christ.*
—RUTHANN RIDLEY

For years my mother hung a print in our living room that depicted Jesus knocking at a heart's door, asking to enter. I never passed through that room, lazed or rushed, without sensing his incessant request. As a child I warmed at the sight of an insistent Savior tacked to our walnut paneling, but with passing time and moving from one house to another, he gradually became the ubiquitous, untiring Christ—always there, always wanting the same thing. Eventually I pitied him, precariously pinned to various walls, unable to focus on anything but that thick, unyielding door. Unable to speak aloud.

However, I figured if our living-room Christ *did* talk audibly to me, he'd be laconic and repetitive. "Come to me," he'd say. "Give all of you to me." On one level that sounded unarguably selfish. I had things to do: drudging to school, squirming through homework, rehabilitating my bedroom, consorting with friends, prowling for clothes, and of course, passing through church doors whenever *they* opened. Did he want me to quit all that? It'd be subhuman. Yet on another level, at an early age I sensed that life wouldn't settle well if I didn't lavish time on Jesus. I loved him and had accepted his gift of salvation. So technically, I'd opened my inner door. But frequently, especially later as a young adult, it felt more like a crack to squeeze through than a swung-wide-open welcome. With unrelenting schedules, burgeoning interests, repeated waywardness, and a distractible nature, how would I ever give all to Jesus?

Essentially, that's the question I've rammed into most of my life. The years seem shorter and busier, with urgencies or exhaustion beckoning, so how do I grow intimate with Christ? I pry the front door open, slide him a chair, but excuse myself from sitting at his feet. He wouldn't mind waiting while I tidy up and finish a few projects, would he? As I flutter, I'm wary about him not staying put, wandering into dirty back rooms and snooping. That would be bad form. That is what I fear most.

But Christ keeps knocking without interruption and without recrimination when a new wound or need evolves that I can't manage with a vacuum or a Palm Pilot, and suddenly I'm levering the hinges off my door. *Blam!* It crashes, I rush out, and there he stands, waiting for me with outstretched arms. That crumbles me. Anyone else would say, "I told you so," or "Why should I help you now?" Yet Christ enfolds me and whispers his love.

That's how I've learned that crisis and pain open the door to intimacy with Christ. I wish I'd taught myself the easy way, leaving the door permanently ajar or proffering him the guest bedroom, plump pillows and all. But I can't reshape the past, and even if I'd been consistent, I'd have probably flapped around with a feather duster in hand. Why can't I just be an adoring disciple, leaning on his breast without care for the morrow?

Oh, Jesus, when will I change? Why do I wait for inner darkness before I crave your light? Thank you for the persistence, for always waiting at my door.

---

*Here I am!*
*I stand at the door and knock.*
*If anyone hears my voice and opens the door,*
*I will come in and eat with him, and he with me.*

—REVELATION 3:20

# Staying at Home

## Brent Curtis

Two years ago, worn out by three years of spiritual battle, I found myself asking: "Jesus, if your Spirit abides in me in the person of the Holy Spirit, who is my Comforter, why do I so often feel alone and you seem so far away?" What came to me in response were Jesus' words in John 15:5, "I am the vine; you are the branches. If a man remains in me and I in him, he will bear much fruit; apart from me you can do nothing." Jesus was saying, "Living spiritually requires something more than just not sinning or doing good works. In order to live in the kingdom of heaven, you must abide in me. Your identity is in me."

*If I'm not abiding in Jesus, then where is it that I abide?* I asked myself.

I began to notice that, when I was tired or anxious, there were certain sentences I would say in my head that led me to a very familiar place. The journey to this place would often start with me walking around disturbed, feeling as if there was something deep inside that I needed to put into words but couldn't quite capture. I felt that "something" as an anxiety, a loneliness, and a need for connection with someone.

If no connection came, I would start saying things like "Life really stinks. Why is it always so hard? It's never going to change." If no one noticed that I was struggling and asked me what was wrong, I found my sentences shifting to a more cynical level: "Who cares? Life is really a joke." Surprisingly, I noticed by the time I was saying those last sentences, I was feeling better. The anxiety was greatly diminished.

■    ■    ■

My "comforter," my abiding place, was cynicism and rebellion. From this abiding place, I would feel free to use some soul cocaine—a violence video with maybe a little titillation thrown in, perhaps having a little more alcohol with a meal than I might normally drink—things that would allow me to feel better for just a little while. I had always thought of these things as just bad habits. I began to see they were much more; they were spiritual abiding places that were my comforters and friends in a very spiritual way; literally, other lovers.

The final light went on one evening when I read John 15 in *The Message*. Eugene Peterson translates Jesus' words on abiding in this way: "If you make yourselves at home with me and my words are at home in you, you can be sure that whatever you ask will be listened to and acted upon." Jesus was saying in answer to my question, "I have made my home in you, Brent. But you still have other comforters you go to. You must learn to make your home in me." I realized that my identity had something to do with simply "staying at home."

It also dawned on me that holiness, surprisingly, also comes not out of doing but out of staying at home, with who and where we are and with who and where God is in us. Indeed, we will only have the courage to leave home and continue to live as pilgrims out on the road if we have some sense that our true home abides within us in the Spirit of Christ and that we can do the same with him. And in the meantime, out of this abiding, Jesus transforms us. Our identity begins to coalesce, not out of doing, but out of living with a good friend for a number of years and simply finding we have become more like him.

—*The Sacred Romance*, 1997

# Looking Up Close

*The world is not yet exhausted;*
*let me see something tomorrow*
*which I never saw before.*

—SAMUEL JOHNSON

This morning I meant to pray for friends and their needs, but instead, buried under blankets to calm the shivers, I hurled disparate complaints at the ceiling. *Why, God, aren't clients paying their invoices? Why does everything seem at a standstill? I'm bored. You don't answer my prayers for healing. I can't shake this oppression. You're ignoring what I want in life. In fact, there are lots of prayers you haven't answered…and why are the heating bills so high and the house so cold?*

God probably anticipated the questions. It's the week of Valentine's Day and my birthday, the days on which I predictably hack apart my life. I'm reminded that I haven't received romantic flowers from a man in years and I'm older and none the wiser—nor closer to my dream of a European vacation. (I can't even afford to fix my aging teeth.) This year I'm not just melancholy. I'm inconsolable. Friends suggest dinner and a movie, and I privately bemoan their lack of imagination, though I can't think of anything creative myself. My surroundings feel dull and provincial. I want to be alone, wishing I could vanish Garbo-esque style, but I could never evince the glamour and mystery; hardly anybody would notice I'd disappeared.

What's wrong with me? Too much sugar? Not enough sleep? Menopause? My friend Madalene might say it's self-pity. Her words would sting with truth, but I'm also weary. When I repeatedly struggle with loss and disappointment, I lurch back and my vision blurs. I can't perceive God's involvement in my life. I strain, looking past the horizon and missing his creativity dotted across the foreground, embedded into a grand scheme like a Pointillism painting. Like my favorite Seurat masterpiece, I need to step forward, scrutinize the artist's technique, and marvel at his detailed precision.

More pragmatically, I need to make lists. They help me recognize what's *there* instead of what's not there. I begin plaintively, compiling my gripes and griefs. (How can I conquer this disturbance if I don't know precisely what torments me?) Then I invite myself—even force myself—to concentrate on general gratitudes. What do I appreciate in my life? This list forms with less celerity than the grievances, but it churns out nonetheless, even if I can only recall Western foregone assumptions like, "I eat three meals a day." (Many people in the world don't.) These gratitudes lighten me a little, but not with the electrifying power that Oprah promotes. *Most everybody I know has these things...even more,* I pout. No, when I'm this downhearted, I need to identify what God has *specifically* done for me. (Selfish, I know, but it's true.) I want evidence of his action on my behalf, the reassurance that he's not abandoned me.

So another list begins, the one that usually stuns and shames me. As I recount God's unique gifts to me, one blinding oversight appears: I've concentrated so severely on the "big picture"—the major miracles that I've pummeled God for and haven't received—that I've obscured his "smaller" blessings. For example, the untangling of someone's gnarly attitude. New, fervent prayer partners for the ministry. An unexpected check slivered into my post office box, just in time to pay the phone bill. Specifically qualified volunteers to assist me with time-consuming administrative tasks. A "chance" meeting with a publisher at a coffeehouse, which produces new work for me. A gift from a long-distance friend that uncannily fulfills a desire she didn't know about. All represent answers to prayer—that God touches the prosaic needs and nuances, despite my unflagging complaints.

At this point I'm embarrassed into repenting of my ingratitude and gathering up my straggling faith. If the Creator painstakingly paints into the cracks and corners of the mundane, he can swash a miracle across the blank sections of my stretched canvas.

---

*And my God will meet all your needs*
*according to his glorious riches in Christ Jesus.*

—PHILIPPIANS 4:19

# Open My Eyes, Lord

## *A Prayer for the Spiritually Weary*

Open my eyes that I may see
wonderful things in your law.
I am a stranger on earth;
do not hide your commands from me....
I am laid low in the dust;
preserve my life according to your word.
I recounted my ways and you answered me;
teach me your decrees.
Let me understand the teaching of your precepts;
then I will meditate on your wonders.
My soul is weary with sorrow;
strengthen me according to your word.
Keep me from deceitful ways;
be gracious to me through your law....
I hold fast to your statutes, O LORD;
do not let me be put to shame.

—PSALM 119:18-19,25-29,31

# Mirrors

*Walter  Wangerin  Jr.*

In mirrors I see myself. But in mirrors made of glass and silver I never see the *whole* of myself. I see the me I want to see, and I ignore the rest.

Mirrors that hide nothing hurt me. They reveal an ugliness I'd rather deny. Yow! Avoid these mirrors of veracity!

My wife is such a mirror. When I have sinned against her, my sin appears in the suffering of her face. Her tears reflect with terrible accuracy my selfishness. My *self!* But I hate the sight, and the same selfishness I see now makes me look away.

"Stop crying!" I command, as though the mirror were at fault. Or else I just leave the room. Walk away.

Oh, what a coward I am, and what a fool! Only when I have the courage fully to look, clearly to know myself—even the evil of myself—will I admit my need for healing. But if I look away from her whom I have hurt, I have also turned away from her who might forgive me. I reject the very source of my healing.

My denial of my sin protects, preserves, perpetuates that sin! Ugliness in me, while I live in illusions, can only grow the uglier.

Mirrors that hide nothing hurt me. But this is the hurt of purging and precious renewal—and these are mirrors of dangerous grace.

■　　■　　■

The passion of Christ, his suffering and his death, is such a mirror. Are the tears of my dear wife hard to look at? Well, the pain in the face of

Jesus is harder. It is my *self* in the extremest truth. My sinful self. The death he died reflects a selfishness so extreme that by it I was divorced from God and life and light completely: I raised my *self* higher than God! But because the Lord God is the only true God, my pride did no more, in the end, than to condemn this false god of my *self* to death. For God will *be* God, and all false gods will fall before him.

So that's what I see reflected in the mirror of Christ's crucifixion: my death. My rightful punishment. My sin and its just consequence. Me. And precisely because it is so accurate, the sight is nearly intolerable.

Nevertheless, I will not avoid this mirror! No, I will carefully rehearse…the passion of my Jesus—with courage, with clarity and faith; for this is the mirror of dangerous grace, purging more purely than any other.

For this one is not made of glass and silver, nor of fallen flesh only. This mirror is made of righteous flesh and of divinity, both—and this one loves me absolutely. My wife did not choose to take my sin and so to reflect my truth to me. She was driven, poor woman. But Jesus did choose—not only to take the sin within himself, not only to reflect the squalid truth of my personal need, but also to reveal the tremendous truth of his face and forgiveness. He took that sin *away.*

This mirror is not passive only, showing what is; it is active, creating new things to be. It shows me a new me behind the shadow of a sinner. For when I gaze at his crucifixion, I see my death indeed—but my death done! His death is the death of the selfish one, whom I called ugly and hated to look upon.

And resurrection is another me.

*—Reliving the Passion, 1992*

# Flat on Our Faces

*Once I turned from thee and hid,*
*Bound on what thou hadst forbid;*
*Sow the wind I would; I sinned:*
*I repent of what I did.*

*Bad I am, but yet thy child.*
*Father, be thou reconciled.*
*Spare thou me, since I see*
*With thy might that thou art mild.*

—GERARD MANLEY HOPKINS

It was a dark and stormy twilight. I pointed my rental car into the parking lot at the beach community, scanning the silhouettes of oddly shaped houses. They'd been constructed more vertical than horizontal, or with singular sections jutting into the sky, so inhabitants could view the ocean over double and triple rows of part-time dwellings. If there hadn't been lousy weather, matched by my bleak mood, the vacation homes would have appeared comical to my landlubber mindset. But instead, they looked ominous, almost surreal. In the whipping wind they reached up for something untouchable, and I knew how futile that felt.

There's something about me and the ocean. Whenever I'm deeply troubled I wind up at the beach. That's quite a feat for somebody like me who's always lived inland and doesn't travel much. But recently a new friend had offered her second home to me for a writing stint, and I grabbed the opportunity. Combined with a free airline ticket and my birthday, it seemed like the perfect inexpensive getaway, a writer's fantasy. And it would have been, if life hadn't dumped on me recently.

Several incidents contributed to my despondency, but the biggest scare arrived from the Internal Revenue Service. For some time it had wanted money I didn't have, and the agency's recent letters frightened me. I'd already exhausted my options and before leaving for the California coast I'd reviewed every inch of my financial life and filled out a compromise proposal to the IRS. Pulling out of denial and facing the facts dismantled me emotionally, and on my birthday I traveled to the beach feeling stricken and isolated. Only God could pull me out of this one, but I didn't think he'd comply. After all, the IRS was right: I'd fallen behind on paying taxes and I needed to deliver. I believed the Lord helped the righteous, but what about the guilty?

There's something about potential disgrace that softens the heart and leads to introspection. I thought a lot about sin and guilt that week and walked the beach repenting of my transgressions. Most of my repentance didn't relate to back taxes, but to other offenses I'd committed, past and present. Suddenly acts and attitudes I'd never considered as sin flared up as grievances against God, and I scrolled through my entire life and the people who'd passed through it, crying and confessing. Back in the house I listed the individuals to whom I needed to apologize, and prayed for their healing and forgiveness.

I didn't write much those days, but God thoroughly scrubbed my soul. Still, I didn't feel condemned; only the Spirit's gentle illumination and nudging toward confession. As I wobbled through the week, my repentance transformed to "getting right with God" rather than getting out of trouble. His pleasure became all that mattered to me. In turn, each day my spirit lightened a bit, though I'd no idea whether the financial dilemma would resolve without the IRS taking extreme measures. I traveled home sensing that with God I could face whatever happened, and later that year I settled peacefully with the tax collectors.

Yes, there's something about pain that opens our spiritual eyes and leads us to repentance. However, we needn't fear when this occurs, for God shows mercy to those who truly feel sorry for their sin and request forgiveness. Not to get themselves out of a pickle, but to surrender and cleanse themselves. Actually, periodically falling flat on our faces before God enhances spiritual sensitivity and effectiveness, drawing us closer into the Maker's heart. This also dislodges an inner door and allows him to pour in grace, forgiveness, and blessing. The circumstances may not change, but our ability to deal with them will. It begins with the prayer, "God, be merciful to me, a sinner."

---

*Repent, then, and turn to God,*
*so that your sins may be wiped out,*
*that times of refreshing*
*may come from the Lord.*

—ACTS 3:19

# Spiritual Ironies

*As sure as ever God puts*
*his children in the furnace,*
*he will be in the furnace with them.*
—CHARLES HADDON SPURGEON

On a recent out-of-town trip, I called a longtime friend, wondering if we could wedge in dinner between my engagements. We hadn't talked face to face for a few years. A weary voice answered the phone, and soon she divulged the startling adversity in her family life. So no, she couldn't get away socially, but she could talk awhile. Then for an hour she described the unending, unbearable pain inflicted on her home.

To divulge more would break a confidence, but her story's overview stunned me into stretches of silence. I asked a few questions, offered my support and sympathy, but it felt like empty platitudes. My friend and her husband are authentic Christians. They've served others with compassion and perseverance and did nothing to deserve their unconscionable circumstances. Yet they die daily.

"I live between the two statements in the book of Job," explained my friend. "On the one hand I want to curse God and die. On the other, though he slay me yet will I trust him." She sighed. "It's like one hand makes a fist and shakes it at God, and the other hand, which is open, pleads to him for help." She inhabits inexplicable spiritual ironies: The God who allows us to suffer is the only One who can deeply comfort us. The Lord who dumps us into the furnace is the only One who can pluck us from the fire. The Provider who falls interminably silent constantly hovers over us. At times the physical evidence says we can't depend on God, but we can't afford not to trust him, either.

Some pain cuts so deep that books, Bible verses, gratitude lists, well-meaning words, and other comforts don't penetrate. They sound silly and simplistic. We can only stand in the fire and wait for the angel.

---

*Why, O LORD, do you stand far off?*
*Why do you hide yourself in times of trouble?*

—PSALM 10:1

# Lost in the Psalms

*The psalms acquire, for those*
*who know how to enter them,*
*a surprising depth, a marvelous*
*and inexhaustible actuality.*
*They are bread, miraculously provided*
*by Christ, to feed those*
*who have followed him*
*into the wilderness.*

—THOMAS MERTON

For the last few years, I've been lost in the psalms, and probably won't forage anywhere else in the Scriptures soon. Crisis and disillusionment need empathy and guidance, and the poetic cries and whispers of David and other psalmists supply ample sustenance if I'm hungry, or edible bits when I'm spiritually anorexic. The psalms' repetition and familiarity offer stability in life's storms; many liturgical Christians will attest to this soothing truth.

I'm not advocating that we skip reading all of the Bible, but when we're rattled and can't handle much else, the psalms provide a nearly "whole food" nourishment more than any other canonized book. God dwells in his Word and meets our variant yearnings there, but he particularly bends to our neediness in the psalms.

"The wide range of expression in the Psalter—the anger and pain of lament, the anguished self-probing of confession, the grateful fervor of thanksgiving, the ecstatic joy of praise—allows us to bring our whole lives to God," writes Kathleen Norris.[8] Yet once we've expressed ourselves, the psalms usher us from self-focus to God's character. Eugene H. Peterson explains, "The psalms are access to an environment in which God is the pivotal center of life, and in which all other people and events are third parties. Neither bane nor blessing distracts the psalmists for long from this center."9

Here's a sampling of why, in these last years, I've gravitated toward the beloved poetry.

When I ache for *comfort:*

> I know, O LORD, that your laws are righteous,
>   and in faithfulness you have afflicted me.
> May your unfailing love be my comfort,
>   according to your promise to your servant.
> Let your compassion come to me that I may live,
>   for your law is my delight.
> May the arrogant be put to shame for wronging
>     me without cause;
>   but I will meditate on your precepts.
>     (Psalm 119:75-78)

When I burst with *complaint:*

> How long, O LORD? Will you forget me forever?
>   How long will you hide your face from me?
> How long must I wrestle with my thoughts
>   and every day have sorrow in my heart?
>   How long will my enemy triumph over me?
>
> Look on me and answer, O LORD my God.
>   Give light to my eyes, or I will sleep in death;
> my enemy will say, "I have overcome him,"
>   and my foes will rejoice when I fall.

But I trust in your unfailing love;
  my heart rejoices in your salvation.
    (Psalm 13:1-5)

## When I seek the Lord's *direction:*

Delight yourself in the LORD
  and he will give you the desires of your heart.

Commit your way to the LORD;
  trust in him and he will do this:
He will make your righteousness shine like
    the dawn,
  the justice of your cause like the noonday sun.

Be still before the LORD and wait patiently
    for him;
  do not fret when men succeed in their ways,
  when they carry out their wicked schemes.
    (Psalm 37:4-7)

## When I stumble toward *repentance:*

Have mercy on me, O God,
  according to your unfailing love;
according to your great compassion
  blot out my transgressions.
Wash away all my iniquity
  and cleanse me from my sin.

For I know my transgressions,
  and my sin is always before me.

Against you, you only, have I sinned
and done what is evil in your sight,
so that you are proved right when you speak
and justified when you judge....

Cleanse me with hyssop, and I will be clean;
wash me, and I will be whiter than snow.
(Psalm 51:1-4,7)

When I falter in *perseverance:*

Cast your cares on the LORD
and he will sustain you;
he will never let the righteous fall.

Away from me, you evildoers,
that I may keep the commands of my God!
Sustain me according to your promise,
and I will live;
do not let my hopes be dashed.
Uphold me, and I will be delivered;
I will always have regard for your decrees.
(Psalm 55:22; 119:115-117)

When I need spiritual *reassurance:*

Blessed is the man
who does not walk in the counsel of the wicked
or stand in the way of sinners
or sit in the seat of mockers.
But his delight is in the law of the LORD,
and on his law he meditates day and night.

He is like a tree planted by streams of water,
which yields its fruit in season
and whose leaf does not wither.
Whatever he does prospers....
For the LORD watches over the way of the righteous,
but the way of the wicked will perish.
(Psalm 1:1-3,6)

Actually, each of the 150 chapters can feed the soul, if we'll open the book and our hearts to its internally astute messages. If we're to lose ourselves to anything, the supernatural psalms prove wiser than most of the earthly options we're enticed toward when stressed.

---

*I wait for the LORD, my soul waits,*
*and in his word I put my hope.*

— PSALM 130:5

# Prayer and Trouble

## E. M. Bounds

In the time of trouble, where does prayer come in? The psalmist tells us: "Call upon me in the day of trouble; I will deliver thee, and thou shalt glorify me." Prayer is the most appropriate thing for a soul to do in the "time of trouble." Prayer recognizes God in the day of trouble. "It is the Lord; let him do what seemeth good." Prayer sees God's hand in trouble, and prays about it. Nothing more surely shows us our helplessness than when trouble comes. It brings the strong man low, it discloses our weakness, it brings a sense of helplessness. Blessed is he who knows how to turn to God in "the time of trouble." If trouble is of the Lord, then the most natural thing to do is carry the trouble to the Lord, and seek grace and patience and submission. It is the time to inquire in the trouble, "Lord, what wilt thou have me to do?" How natural and reasonable for the soul, oppressed, broken, and bruised, to bow low at the footstool of mercy and seek the face of God? Where could a soul in trouble more likely find solace than in the closet?

Alas! trouble does not always drive men to God in prayer. Sad is the case of him who, when trouble bends his spirit down and grieves his heart, yet knows not whence the trouble comes nor knows how to pray about it. Blessed is the man who is driven by trouble to his knees in prayer!

Prayer in the time of trouble brings comfort, help, hope, and blessings, which, while not removing the trouble, enable the saint the better to bear it and to submit to the will of God. Prayer opens the eyes to see

God's hand in trouble. Prayer does not interpret God's providences, but it does justify them and recognize God in them. Prayer enables us to see wise ends in trouble. Prayer in trouble drives us away from unbelief, saves us from doubt, and delivers from all vain and foolish questionings because of our painful experiences. Let us not lose sight of the tribute paid to Job when all his trouble came to the culminating point: "In all this Job sinned not, nor charged God foolishly."

Alas! for vain, ignorant men, without faith in God and knowing nothing of God's disciplinary process in dealing with men, who charge God foolishly when trouble comes, and who are tempted to "curse God." How silly and vain are the complainings, the murmurings and the rebellion of men in the time of trouble! What need to read again the story of the children in the wilderness! And how useless is all our fretting, our worrying over trouble, as if such unhappy doings on our part could change things! "And which of you with taking thought, can add to his stature one cubit?" How much wiser, much better, how much easier to bear life's trouble when we take everything to God in prayer?

Trouble has wise ends for the praying ones, and these find it so. Happy is he who, like the psalmist, finds that his troubles have been blessings in disguise. "It is good for me that I have been afflicted, that I might learn thy statutes. I know, O Lord, that thy judgments are right, and that thou in faithfulness has afflicted me."

— *The Essentials of Prayer, 1925*

# A New Definition
# of Love

*Love is the result of an identification—*
*the identifying of our wills*
*with the will of God.*

—ROSE TERLIN

When Ali McGraw chastised Ryan O'Neal with "Love is never having to say you're sorry," I swooned with the teens of my generation who stampeded to the movie *Love Story.* This film logic appealed to me, influencing my outlook on love in young adulthood. Love should be fun and passionate and reckless. Love needn't apologize, criticize the other person, or pass through hardship. Unless, of course, somebody like Ali's character died, but that engendered enough pathos to sound wildly romantic and preserved the stricken lover as forever young and flawless.

Unfortunately, this definition collided with the Bible's teaching about God's loving character. I'd read that God is love, and that we can know and rely on his love for us (1 John 4:16). That sounded generous and satisfying, but to me it didn't jibe with what Jesus taught about love. In fact, God's Son sounded self-centered. For example: "If you love me, you will obey what I command" (John 14:15). His followers didn't cure my crippled viewpoint, either. The writer of Hebrews announced, "The Lord disciplines those he loves, and he punishes everyone he accepts as a son" (Hebrews 12:6).

Obedience and discipline: How could they be loving? Why would God inflict these unsavories on his beloved? Decades later I'm still prone to sputter those questions, but I'm slowly—with the speed of a snail—comprehending the truth that compliance and hardship intertwine with love. From God's standpoint, he asks us to obey so we can live purely and with less woundedness. He applies discipline—the pressure of pain and behaving contrary to our desires—to heal and demolish what ultimately ruins us. That is his loving will; this is what he'll relentlessly pursue all our lives. He wants us to be better, live better, and act like his Son, the model of unfettered wholeness.

So in the last years, though squirming and complaining and whimpering, I've gradually acquiesced. Because God loves me, he wants to correct my character flaws—problems like my covert pride, razor wit, critical spirit, unbridled ambition, unaccountable spending, and nonexistent discipline. (There's more, but those admissions alone could potentially humble me to the public the rest of my life.) It requires obedience and discipline, pain and struggle, to chip into the core of these vulgarities and supplant them with the "peaceable fruit of righteousness" (Hebrews 12:11, KJV).

Occasionally I glimpse the notion of snuggling under the cloak of peaceful righteousness, and I like it. One day I guided my car into the driveway and thought, *What's this strange feeling that I have?* Immediately the words slipped into mind: the peaceable fruit of righteousness. *This is what it's like to let go of sin—it's peaceful!* After mentally kicking and screaming through a problem area, I'd laid it down, and God had blessed me with serenity. Except, inner calmness felt so foreign to me, I didn't recognize it. I was accustomed to noisily galumphing barely ahead of my sin, afraid of its pointy guilt-exposing finger.

"The heart is deceitful above all things and beyond cure [without God]. Who can understand it?" (Jeremiah 17:9). I don't understand my sinful interior. Despite all I've learned, why do I still do what I don't want to do? Why do I do what's not good for me? God knows the answers, and he chastens what disables me. Not so he can love me, but *because* he loves me. I don't know if I'll ever completely cooperate, but I am reworking my definition of love to match his. Maybe I'm growing up.

---

*No discipline seems pleasant at the time, but painful.*
*Later on, however, it produces a harvest of righteousness*
*and peace for those who have been trained by it.*

—HEBREWS 12:11

# Messengers
# in Strange Places

*Kind words are the music of the world.*
*They have a power which seems*
*to be beyond natural causes,*
*as though they were some angel's song*
*which had lost its way and come to earth.*

— FREDERICK WILLIAM FABER

About halfway through a low-income month, I decided to escort another valuable item to the pawn shop as collateral for a loan. I mention "another item" because already my diamond earrings and necklace, sapphire ring, and fax machine resided there until I earned enough money to bail them out. The year before I'd lost all of my emerald jewelry—two rings, studded earrings, a tennis bracelet—to another pawn shop because I couldn't gather up enough cash to redeem them in time. Consequently, approaching such places represented temporary relief but long-term risk to me.

At the same time, I didn't have other options for paying bills. Nor much else left worth pawning, except my computer—which, bottom line, I needed to keep for work—and the copy machine. I sighed, unplugged the copier's cord, and lugged it into the most valuable thing I own, my Kia Sportage, which thankfully can't be pawned because I'm still making payments on it.

I must have looked forlorn because the pawn shop clerk sparred with the manager to loan me the most cash possible. The clerk talked kindly to me, though, as he handed me papers to fill out. I knew the routine: name, address, phone number. Yes, I owned the item. No, I hadn't stolen it. Then as I handed the paperwork back to this new ally, he probed into my eyes and whispered, "You know, everything's going to be all right."

I teared up. Somebody knew what I needed to hear and dared to say it. I thanked him, took the cash, and walked quietly but appreciatively out the door. It's interesting—I've visited that shop several times since then, but I've never seen the kind clerk again. Was he an angel?

When we need reassurance, God might send us comforting messengers, but sometimes they're in unexpected and strange places. Try not to miss them.

---

*As a mother comforts her child,*
*so will I comfort you.*

—ISAIAH 66:13

# PART SIX

# More Temptations

Just when we begin to understand and embrace the process of brokenness, temptation strikes. Something happens that discourages us. We want to give up, turn back, forget the growth, stomp out the pain. But those who look back turn into pillars of salt, useless for the kingdom and lifeless versions of their true selves.

We can recognize "easy outs" for what they are: a dark enemy who lividly opposes our spiritual progress. We can cultivate the spiritual resources to recognize his tactics and overcome them.

# The Lure of Egypt

## *Jamie Buckingham*

God never brings a hindrance into our lives that He does not intend to be used to open another door that would not have opened otherwise.

When God spoke to Moses at the burning bush at the base of Mt. Sinai, commissioning him to return to Egypt to lead the Israelites out of bondage, He had a clear-cut plan. He said He was concerned about the suffering of the Israelites. He said He had to come to rescue them and to take care of them as they traveled, and that He would bring them to Mt. Sinai to worship Him (Exodus 3:7-12).

But such promises are hard to remember when you run out of water in the desert.

In Exodus 15:25, the historical account says the Lord was testing the people at Marah. In the Western concept, testing is for the purpose of ascertaining knowledge. It is used to determine how much one has learned. But the biblical concept of testing is not to ascertain knowledge; it is a method of teaching. When God "tests" His people, He is not doing so to find out whether they have learned their lesson and deserve a good grade. God's tests are learning experiences, designed by the Teacher to share knowledge, not to determine its presence or absence.

Thus, when God tested the people at Marah, He did it with a decree, not a questionnaire. It is a marvelous promise that, like all God's promises, is conditional—found in the subjunctive mood and preceded by an *if.* The promise of the absence of disease is for those who (1) listen carefully to the voice of the Lord; (2) do what is right in His eyes; (3) pay attention to His commands; and (4) keep all His decrees. Only then does a person have the right to claim the promise of "none of these diseases."

An old Bible teacher used to remind his pupils that, not only was the Lord interested in getting the people out of Egypt, He also wanted to get Egypt out of the people. That, perhaps, is at the heart of all wilderness experiences. In this case, the people brought a lot of Egypt with them—internally. Now at Marah, the Lord spoke and told them He would not allow the Egyptian disease to afflict them—if they but obeyed Him.

What did God want the Israelites to do? Obviously, He wanted them to drink the water of Marah. But it was filled with magnesium. True, but even Moses could not have known about the medicinal qualities of calcium and magnesium. For one thing, magnesium is a powerful laxative. It was God's way of cleaning out their systems. Had they drunk the bitter water, and continued to drink it despite its effects on their intestines, their bodies would have ceased the purgative action and grown accustomed to the water. In the process, however, they would have expelled most of the amoebae, parasites, and death-dealing germs they brought with them from Egypt.

There is another medicinal quality about the water of Marah. Calcium and magnesium form the basis of a drug called *dolomite.* Dolomite pills are used by professional athletes who perform in the sun. It is basically a muscle control drug to be used in extremely hot weather [to control spasms].

Over and over we are reminded that the reason for wilderness experiences is purification and preparation. The water of Marah would have certainly brought almost instant purification. God was about to change the entire eating structure of the nation. No longer would they gorge themselves on shellfish, pork, and the highly spiced foods of Egypt. To accomplish this change, God started with a purge, ridding the Israelites of all their perverse yearnings and desires. He was about to introduce them to their new dietary structure known ever since as "kosher." But the people rebelled at the first test. Thus the promise of a people without diseases had to wait for a generation who listened carefully to the voice of the Lord and did not grumble at His commands.

The principle holds true even today. God wants us not only to live, but to live abundantly. So He continually leads us back to the water of Marah where our crusty spirits may be broken—and the Spirit of God may enter.

*        *        *

God had a keen ear. It is especially tuned to those caught in desert experiences, for God does not allow His children to experience the wilderness without purpose. Even the changing of our diet from meat to manna is part of God's greater plan for our lives.

God has a purpose for everything He does. There was purpose in the manna. Granted, manna was not what they ordered off God's menu. They wanted the food of Egypt. Yet God's ways are not our ways. His provision often looks superficial to the carnal mind. "If we were God's 'chosen people,' why do we have such a meager diet? We should eat like kings—like the pharaoh."

It was the sin of presumption, for they felt they knew better than God what they should eat. They were too shortsighted to understand a God who insisted on closing the door to Egypt's food forever, and who was more interested in teaching them the discipline of obedience than in satisfying their carnal cravings.

When Moses refused to listen to their grumbling and requests to turn back, they rebelled. It was, in essence, a counterrevolution—a common problem faced by all revolutionary leaders whose followers, after their first victories, often grow discouraged over the sparse diet and long trek before reaching the Promised Land.

God prescribed a strict diet of manna along with restrictions for gathering and storing. It was more than many could take. It's not that they wanted to return to bondage; they just wanted a quick respite into the past—an overnight excursion, so to speak, back to sin.

But such excursions are always forbidden by God, for they bring with them a rekindling of old tastes for things not healthy. Manna was not tasty. But God was changing tastes. He was transforming a group of sloppy, undisciplined former slaves into an army. There is no place for gourmet menus in the wilderness. Here people exist on bare essentials—getting their minds off their bellies and onto God.

The manna of God was to be only temporary. Just a few days ahead lay the Promised Land with milk, wine, and honey. Only further disobedience caused God to have to keep the manna coming—for forty years.

The carnal appetite, which God was burning from them with His prescribed diet, is never satisfied. It always yearns for more. It causes people to run after every new "prophet" who comes on the scene with a "new revelation" from God. It causes them to trade the written Word of God for the philosophy of the world since it seems more palatable. It causes people to demand melons and meat while disdaining what God has placed before them.

But the only way to reach the Promised Land is by eating God's diet. Leeks, onions, and garlic will not get you into Canaan, for that diet is always accompanied by the bondage of Egypt. In the wilderness we must make priority decisions. Are we willing to give up what satisfies the belly to have what satisfies the soul?

Those who ignore or refuse God's provision while lusting for the former things (which the Bible says must eventually be "put away") will soon perish and be burned in the sands of the wilderness—the very place where God's manna which they rejected covered the earth.

Yet the others—those who accept God's meager diet on faith, believing God has a purpose for what He serves up—enter into a marvelous truth that lean diets are intended only for a season. To those who obey and do not grumble, there lies ahead a table in the wilderness. Here, then, is the truth: While we are in the wilderness, we are not of the wilderness. We are bound for the Promised Land.

*— A  Way  Through  the  Wilderness,  1983*

# Grace

## *Kathleen Norris*

Jacob's theophany, his dream of angels on a stairway to heaven, strikes me as an appealing tale of unmerited grace. Here's a man who has just deceived his father and cheated his brother out of an inheritance. But God's response to finding Jacob vulnerable, sleeping all alone in open country, is not to strike him down for his sins but to give him a blessing.

Jacob wakes from the dream in awe, exclaiming, "Surely the Lord is in this place—and I did not know it!" For once, his better instincts take hold, and he responds by worshiping God. He takes the stone that he'd kept close by all night, perhaps to use as a weapon if a wild animal, or his furious brother Esau, were to attack him, and sets it up as a shrine, leaving it for future travelers, so that they, too, will know that this is a holy place, the dwelling place of God.

Jacob's exclamation is one that remains with me, a reminder that God can choose to dwell everywhere and anywhere we go. One morning this past spring, I noticed a young couple with an infant at an airport departure gate. The baby was staring intently at other people, and as soon as he recognized a human face, no matter whose it was, no matter if it was young or old, pretty or ugly, bored or happy or worried-looking he would respond with absolute delight.

It was beautiful to see. Our drab departure gate had become the gate of heaven. And as I watched that baby play with any adult who would allow it, I felt as awe-struck as Jacob, because I realized that this is how God looks at us, staring into our faces in order to be delighted, to see the creature he made and called good, along with the rest of creation. And, as Psalm 139 puts it, darkness is as nothing to God, who can look right through whatever evil we've done in our lives to the creature made in the divine image.

I suspect that only God, and well-loved infants, can see this way. But it gives me hope to think that when God gazed on the sleeping Jacob, he looked right through the tough little schemer and saw something good, if only a capacity for awe, for recognizing God and worshiping. That Jacob will worship badly, trying to bargain with God, doesn't seem to matter. God promises to be with him always.

Peter denied Jesus, and Saul persecuted the early Christians, but God could see the apostles they would become. God does not punish Jacob as he lies sleeping because he can see in him Israel, the foundation of a people. God loves to look at us, and loves it when we look back at him. Even when we try to run away from our troubles, as Jacob did, God will find us, and bless us, even when we feel most alone, unsure if we'll survive the night. God will find a way to let us know that he is with us *in this place,* wherever we are, however far we think we've run. And maybe that's one reason we worship—to respond to grace. We praise God not to celebrate our own faith but to give thanks for the faith God has in us. To let ourselves look at God, and let God look back at us. And to laugh, and sing, and be delighted because God has called us his own.

—*Amazing Grace,* 1998

# The Escape Hatch

*When I speak of a person growing in grace,*
*I mean simply this—that his sense*
*of sin is becoming deeper, his faith stronger,*
*his hope brighter, his love more extensive,*
*and his spiritual-mindedness more marked.*

—BISHOP J. C. RYLE

After wearing my only pair of jeans for three consecutive days, something inside me snapped. Though I couldn't afford it, I just *had* to purchase more casual pants for myself. Invoices clamored for payment, but I stomped on my conscience with excuses: tiny frayed holes peeked through my jeans' pockets, I needed to look better traversing the community, and it'd lift my dulled spirits. I drove to a department store, swept through the Liz Claiborne section, selected three pair of jeans (light blue, dark blue, pitch black; a girl needs variety), wrote a check, and sped to the office to write more chapters about letting God change me through hardship.

I arrived home late that evening, tossed the jeans into the washer and then the dryer, and crawled into bed. The next morning, smug that I'd look fashionable, I pulled on the light blue jeans. They didn't fit right: the crotch and pant legs hung too long. I tried on the dark blue jeans: same misfit. Ditto for the black pair. I checked the labels and couldn't pinpoint the problem. The size was correct, and Liz's jeans *always* fit me well. Finally I rummaged my old jeans from the laundry bag and checked that label.

It stared up at me mockingly: I'd purchased three pairs of *short* jeans, and the old pair was a *petite*. That sounds the same, but it's enough difference to make me feel like a baggy candidate for the clown circus. Compulsion shoved me past trying on the jeans in the store, and I'd already removed the labels and laundered the pants, so they couldn't be returned. All those crisp jeans and nothing to wear.

Perhaps the hardest task God has assigned me is to reduce my spending to manage this pared-down lifestyle. And when I'm worried and pressured and tired of the sacrifice, I'm tempted to purchase niceties to feel better about myself and my storage-unit existence. The denim debacle isn't the only time Satan has triumphed on this battlefront. I like art, books, clothes, furniture, home decorations, office equipment, gardening tools—there's much out there to lure me. So it's a constant, deliberate confrontation with the enemy to keep within slim financial boundaries. Sometimes I win, sometimes I don't, and when I fail I agonize over it privately. *Shouldn't I be farther along spiritually? Shouldn't I better identify the pushy, compulsive marks of the devil?*

It'd be wonderful if I could defeat him every time, but through my experiences, the downfalls of God-loving friends, and the transparent Scriptures, I've concluded that temptation will dwell with us as long as Satan roams the earth. We're especially entranced during difficulty because we yearn for release, if just for moments. The enemy whispers, *Why not just do it? God isn't helping you. He only wants you to suffer. Go ahead, grab a few moments of pleasure. Other people do much worse things than you do.* He tempts the alcoholic to drink, the teen shopper to overspend, the mother to binge on prescription drugs, the husband to dial up pornography on the Internet. Yet simultaneously, God speaks his grace and ways of escape to us, if we choose not to drown out his voice with our internal clamoring.

Paul exhorted the Christians in Corinth, a decadent and sin-drenched city, that "No temptation has seized you except what is common to man. And God is faithful; he will not let you be tempted beyond what you can bear. But when you are tempted, he will also provide a way out so that you can stand up under it" (1 Corinthians 10:13). Practically, that translates to God's providing an escape hatch: a way to run from the temptation. This may be as simple as walking out of the store, as impractical as giving away the computer, as life-changing as switching jobs, or sometimes, as embarrassing as a naked Joseph fleeing from Potiphar's wife (Genesis 39:6-12). We may need to implore a friend to yank us out, receive prayer for deliverance at church, or pay for a therapist's individual or group sessions, but there's a way to escape if we ask God to reveal it—and we look for it.

We can also remember that God hears our repentance and extends his grace. "[God's grace is] for anyone who's ever despaired over sin. This is the removal of our mountain of indebtedness. If you've ever felt that gap between reality and who you're called to be, ever felt like you can't close it—this is grace for you," writes John Ortberg. "God took our indebtedness and guilt and nailed it to the cross. He erased the bill, destroyed the IOU, so you are free. Unburdened. Cleansed. You can live with a heart as light as a feather. Today—no matter what you did yesterday. This is the wonder of grace."[10]

I can't submit this graceful wisdom from my sterling record, but rather, from the truth and reliability of Scripture. And what God says, he will do.

---

*Through these he has given us his very great*
*and precious promises, so that through them*
*you may participate in the divine nature*
*and escape the corruption*
*in the world caused by evil desires.*

—2 PETER 1:4

# Costly Comparisons

*If you share secretly in the joy of someone you envy,*
*you will be freed from your jealousy;*
*and you will also be freed from your jealousy*
*if you keep silent about the person you envy.*

—THALASSIOS THE LIBYAN

I didn't expect the church service to be anything more than the usual Sunday morning fare. Predictably late I slipped into a chair, sang a few upbeat songs, and nodded as the pastor's wife announced our congregation's need for organized intercession. For some reason I felt unusually confident that morning because I introduced myself to a visitor during the meet-and-greet time instead of feeling slightly awkward and introverted and sticking to myself.

"You look familiar to me," I told her, leaning across empty chairs to speak above the chatter. "Do I know you?"

She smiled and replied, "I'm your bank teller."

*Oh, yeah. She's the one who deposits my checks.*

"I'm sorry. I didn't recognize you out of context. You need to be standing behind a counter and looking more banklike," I joked with embarrassment.

"It's okay," she assured me and shifted the Bible in her lap. I realized I'd left my Bible at home—again—and thought about the personal checks I'd bounced recently. *Would she know about them?*

"The pastor's teaching helps me a lot," I commented before she could ask the customary "What do you do?" question. I didn't want to tell her. *Christian Author Bounces Checks* flashed through my mind; it wasn't news I wanted anyone to spread. Just then the congregants re-assembled and I escaped divulging myself, ready to hide behind that week's sermon.

I don't remember why, but my pastor began with an overview of his life and ministry in the context of talking about God's goodness. After several stories he launched into a self-effacing explanation of his success as a published author.

"In school I didn't like English class or writing," he explained with a grin, then admitted he'd received nearly failing grades on his high school and college term papers. "I couldn't even cheat right," he confessed. "Once I hired a guy to write a paper for me and I still earned a D," he laughed. The congregation roared. My spirit suddenly sank.

The pastor continued to recall how a woman in the congregation pestered him to write a book until he couldn't stand the pressure anymore. "Now my book is a best seller on prayer," he announced, "but I can't take the credit for it. It's the Lord's blessing."

With those words my body cranked into motion on its own. My right arm grabbed my purse, my torso thrust upward, and my legs wobbled down the aisle toward the exit—in the middle of the sermon. *What am I doing?* my brain asked. *Isn't this rude? I just got here, and now I'm leaving. What will the bank woman think?* By then I'd reached the foyer where I burst into tears.

I sobbed while driving home, pummeling God with questions, as if he wasn't familiar with the scenario. *Lord, why does he get a best seller—and with his first book? I'm trained as a writer. It's my life calling, but after writing lots of books I'm still struggling. My stuff sells modestly, and I can barely pay the bills. If you're blessing my pastor, then are you cursing me?*

Grief oozed up and smattered more questions. "Why can't I prosper too?" I asked nobody while attempting to fix lunch but couldn't. "I've worked hard and where has it gotten me?" It felt like I'd earned nothing—a big, fat zero. Should I just give up? Who wants a God who doles out zilch?

After crying on and off for an hour, exhausted and disappointed I fell asleep on the living room couch for the afternoon. I didn't attend church for three weeks.

※    ※    ※

I really wasn't mad at my pastor. I admire his spiritual faithfulness, and each week his sermons revive me. He deserves his publishing success and the rewards attached to it. But I *was* frustrated with God, and comparing myself to a reluctant-to-write preacher exposed my bottled-up disappointment. If a pressure cooker isn't vented at least a little, the lid blows off and junk splatters everywhere. So does simmering emotion when it's capped too long.

I'd certainly been capped. Trying to be the "good Christian author" and afraid of what friends, fans, and foes might think, I kept plugging along, stuffing down the pain of unfulfilled hopes and needs. Unwittingly I'd swallowed the message that spiritual maturity—doing everything "right" in God's eyes—equals financial prosperity. After several years as a full-time writer I needed to reconsider that theology, flee to a monastery where money doesn't matter, or just keep working and waiting.

I knew of at least three authors in my church whose books sold well, and no matter how I justified myself, my "numbers" (a publisher's term for sales figures) didn't stack up anywhere near theirs. Never mind that I'd written and compiled more books than all three authors combined. I still belonged to the starving artist category. Once I told one of these authors the average sales numbers for my books and she responded with silence. I might as well have been wearing the sign, Must Be Doing Something Wrong Spiritually. (Actually, it's not fair to assume that she judged me, but she *was* quiet and my insecurity filled in the blank.)

Some would claim my first mistake was comparing myself with someone. I'd say that depends. Comparisons aren't all bad. They uncork bottled emotions that seep into spirits and erode bodies, reminding us that it's healthy to be honest. They prompt us take note, ask questions, wrestle the truth. We can evaluate what we're doing well and what beckons for improvement. We can ask, "What needs to change and how can I change it?" We can create or reaffirm our spiritual definitions. For example, when the emotion subsided I asked myself, "Is success how much money I rake in or whether I follow God's call?" The recesses of my heart still believed the latter. So I'd just have to ignore those who tried to convince me otherwise.

Comparisons also challenge us to mature. I admired my pastor. So could I be happy for him and not feel sorry for myself? The Bible says to rejoice with those who rejoice and mourn with those who mourn (Romans 12:15). I regained some self-respect when I realized I could be thankful for my spiritual leader's blessings while those particular benefits eluded me. It's possible to harbor gladness and sadness together, expressing one emotion without betraying the other. Without insisting that somebody suffers for what we desire but don't possess. But it takes awareness and work. It's not a natural tendency or usually our first thought.

In light of that fact, God gave me some extra credit work on this concept. The week I moved out of my home and into a room at a friend's place, I attended a meeting at Laurel's home. Stepping in the front door I sucked in my breath. Her place looked beautiful, every detail carefully appointed, every room a décor I'd love to own myself. As she showed me around, each room accentuated my loss. I longed for a lovely home of my own, but I had just packed up and placed most of my possessions in storage. Somehow I managed not to expose my feelings and left figuring that was that. I didn't know Laurel very well and probably wouldn't be back.

When I returned to my "new" home that evening, I poured a glass of Chardonnay and sulked on the back deck with my cat Wolfie. I drank a little, cried a lot, and wondered if I'd live in a small unadorned room the rest of my life. Surprisingly, the next morning I felt the Spirit nudging me to call Laurel. I sensed she felt depressed and I was supposed to listen to her.

*You've got to be kidding,* I thought. *She's the one with the great house. She should be consoling me.* However, I knew from experience that I'd miss out on something important if I didn't contact her. I dialed her number and ever since we've been friends. If I'd wallowed in self-pity (something I'm quite good at) I'd have missed out on a creative, inspiring friendship, filled with laughter and thoughtfulness. Today our relationship transcends who lives in which house. With the Lord's enabling, it's possible to enjoy in others what we lack ourselves. Believe me, if I can do it, anyone can. I'm not that virtuous, but God's a miracle worker.

■   ■   ■

If we don't allow comparisons to assess, expand, and improve ourselves, then we're in trouble. Envy moves in and starts gnawing. When we perpetually envy people, it slowly and insidiously erodes us mentally, spiritually, emotionally, and physically. We may think we're hurting them (and we may be), but mostly we're harming ourselves. We expose ourselves as petty, critical, small-minded people. Frederick Buechner defines envy as "the consuming desire to have everybody else be as unsuccessful as you are."[11] It's the awful truth.

Even more, we open ourselves to Satan's influence, which never leads anywhere but spiraling downward. We approach the world with jaundiced eyes and bitter hearts. Eventually we can grow so resentful we cave in on ourselves. Comparisons can be costly.

On the other hand, when we pass through difficult times, it's inevitable that we'll compare and feel tempted to envy. We'll miss what we once had, or what we've never had, and wonder if God flung our desires to the far edges of the universe, never to be recovered. We want to scream and accuse and covet. We're raw and wounded, desiring what we can't seem to possess. What can we do?

It's time to cast ourselves on God and beg for mercy. We can ask him to forgive, cleanse, and renew us. Only he can build our inner resources so we can resist temptation and stave off pity. "And so the power to become sons of God does not come from trying with our human will to act in a godly manner...we are changed by the inward actions of *grace*," explained John of the Cross. "Grace gives us the courage, strength, and boldness to let our old way of seeing things and our past way of dealing with life be put to death. Grace opens the eyes of the soul to the high holiness and beauty and transcendent wisdom of God—the way of life that is above. Then, in spirit, we learn how to live and to 'walk' above every natural event—those that torment and confuse us."[12] Or those that make us compare and complain!

---

*A heart at peace gives life to the body,*
*but envy rots the bones.*

—PROVERBS 14:30

# The Gift of Nothing

## Oswald Chambers

The word of the Lord came to Abraham in a vision. God's method always seems to be vision first then reality, but in between the vision and the reality there is often a deep valley of humiliation.…

Whenever God gives a vision to a saint, he puts the saint in the shadow of his hand and the saint's duty is to be still and listen.… [There is] danger in listening to "good advice" in the dark instead of waiting for God to send the light.

When God gives a vision and darkness follows, wait. God will bring you into accordance with the vision he has given you, if you will await his timing. Otherwise, you try to do away with the supernatural in God's undertakings. Never try to help God fulfill his word. There are some things we cannot do, and that is one of them.

We must never try to anticipate the actual fulfillment of a vision. Often we transact some business spiritually with God on our moment of transfiguration and by faith see clearly a vision of his purpose; then immediately afterward there is nothing but blank darkness. We trust in the Lord, but we walk in darkness.

At that point we are tempted to work up enthusiasm. Instead, we are to wait on God.… When God puts the dark of "nothing" into our experience, it is the most positive "something" he can give to us. If we do anything at that point it is sure to be wrong. We need to stay in the center of nothing and say "thank you" for it. When God gives us nothing it means we are inside him, and by determining to do something we put ourselves outside him. This is a great lesson that few of us seem to learn.

Abraham would not stay in the land when the famine came because there was nothing; he would not trust God for a child because there was no one. God kept giving Abraham nothing (except himself), and by determining to do "something" Abraham jumped outside God and found that he was putting himself in the relationship of the Everlasting No.

There are things God tells us to do without any light or illumination other than the word of his command. All of God's commands are enablings. We must not be weak in his strength.

■   ■   ■

Abraham had anticipated the purpose of God and had to pass through a long time of discipline. The act of Abraham and Sarah [creating a child with Hagar] produced a complexity in God's plan that echoed down through the ages. In the same way, Moses had to wait forty years after his presumptuous attempt to reach his destination.

Adam and Eve did the same thing when they tried to take the "shortcut" (which is the meaning of temptation) and anticipated their destination to be *actually* what they were *potentially* and thereby went wrong. *Temptation does not spring from selfish lust, but from the passionate desire to reach God's destination.*

Abraham emerged out of this stage of discipline with one determination: to let God have his way. There is no indication that he is relying on the flesh any longer; his reliance is on God alone. All self-sufficiency has been destroyed. There is not one common-sense ray left as to how God is going to fulfill his word.

God never hastens and he never tarries. He works his plans out in his own way, and we either lie like clogs in his hands or we assist him by being clay in the hands of the Potter.

Now Abraham sees the real God, not a vision. Such knowledge of the real God is reached when our confidence is placed in God and not in his blessings. Abraham's faith became a tried faith built on a real God.

— *Not Knowing Whither*, 1939

# Jagged Lines

*He who believes himself to be*
*far advanced in the spiritual life*
*has not even made a good beginning.*
—BISHOP JEAN PIERRE CAMUS

In my late twenties, only months after reviving from several spiritually defunct years, somebody asked me to teach a women's Bible study. Immediately I refused. *I can't possibly do that. It hasn't been that long since I've returned to God,* I thought. But the invitation persisted and I started to create a six-week course on basic Christianity.

About five minutes into my preparation for the first lesson, I got stuck. I didn't know how to introduce myself and share my spiritual story. Did the women expect a spiritual giant to teach them? Then already I was sunk, considering my recent inconsistent and rebellious approach to God. I worried about credibility.

*Well, how about being honest?* The question shot at me from nowhere, and I decided that was all I *could* do. I rolled out a long sheet of craft paper, turned it horizontally, and drew a timeline of my spiritual history. Obviously, the line didn't climb steadily upward or even lie flat. My timeline veered up and down, with sharp peaks and valleys, representing repeated spiritual defections, indifferences, or revivals. I labeled the changes in the line with the events that precipitated them: accepted Christ as Savior at five years old; attended a denominational summer camp in junior high; grew disillusioned with my church in high school; broke up with my boyfriend in college; faced my father's death when I was twenty. All of these events affected my relationship with God, and the jagged line told no lie.

I figured once the women reviewed my unabashed inventory, they'd ask for another teacher and I'd be off the didactic hook. That didn't happen. After I told my story, I asked each person to draw a spiritual timeline of her own, then share it with the group. To my surprise every chart jagged up and down, with more lows than highs, like a weather report we'd grumble about. I realized that my vulnerability established an atmosphere in which participants could be honest, and they liked me for it. Some even thanked me. These women *wanted* a teacher who understood the thrills and spills of a spiritual amusement park ride. *Good grief,* I thought. *People are right when they say God can use anybody.*

Twenty years later I also think it's correct to assume that most Christians' spiritual journeys progress on a ragged rather than a streamlined path. We take two steps forward, three steps back. We learn, then contradict what we've learned. We sin and need forgiveness; we grow discouraged and need refreshment. (If that isn't true, then why does the Bible contain so many scriptures about repentance and spiritual renewal for believers?) Humans digress and backslide, and that's what makes God's grace so amazing.

This especially applies when we're traveling through difficult circumstances. It's usually uncharted territory and we choose wrong turns and detours. One day we're mad at God, the next we love him wholeheartedly and beg for his help. Some days we feel emotionless. Wouldn't it be great if we could be honest about these shifts, without fear of judgment? Wouldn't it be wonderful if we accepted fallbacks as part of the spiritual journey and helped people through the rough spots instead of abandoning them? (There are believers who cultivate this honesty among themselves, but they still seem rare. Most Christians I know feel pressured to hide their faults and downfalls.)

One Sunday at church I looked around during the worship time and concluded that everyone but me existed on a spiritual high. They all looked so happy. Then after the sermon our pastor gave an altar call for those who felt discouraged, and most of the congregation stepped forward for prayer. Masks fell off and the ministry team received a generous dose of reality.

■   ■   ■

I've a fantasy about Christians "getting real" in their weekly church services. Rather than testifying about our triumphs, we'd admit to struggles and failures in an atmosphere of acceptance and encouragement. A person could admit things like: "I yelled at my kids as we drove to church. I don't know why I'm so angry." "I lied to my boss." "I'm a recovering alcoholic, but today I feel like drinking." "I know I'm way too materialistic for a Christian, but it's hard not to be that way in my neighborhood!" The other congregants would gather around each struggler and respond with support: "How can we help you through this?" "God loves you so much, even when you fail, and so do we." "We've done that too." "How can we pray for you right now?" There'd be tears and laughter, words of comfort and reassurance. Later everyone would leave without fear of people criticizing or gossiping about them later. During the week they'd pray for and send notes of encouragement to one another.

We may never feel that safe and vulnerable in groups, so it helps to befriend somebody who understands the spurts, pauses, and slips of spiritual growth. Someone with whom we can be honest and accepted, comforted and challenged. When we slide down a few notches, a few poignant critics—sometimes those closest to us—might claim we haven't progressed at all, that we're a hopeless, changeless case. To counter these accusations we need someone who'll prompt us to step back from our personal timeline to view the overall direction of growth. If the line, though filled with jags and downturns, moves ever upward, that's what counts. Is our walk with God better than a year ago, five years ago? That's spiritual growth.

Remember Moses' murder of the Egyptian? David's affair with Bathsheba? The disciples' abandonment of Jesus at the cross? God didn't cast away these backsliders. He forgave, restored, and blessed them with exalted names in Christian history. If he doesn't give up on us when we sin, then why would we?

———————

*I will save them from all their sinful backsliding,*
*and I will cleanse them. They will be my people,*
*and I will be their God.*

—EZEKIEL 37:23

# Momentary Failures

## *Hannah Whitall Smith*

A sudden failure is no reason for being discouraged and giving up all as lost. Neither is the integrity of our doctrine touched by it. We are not preaching a *state,* but a *walk.* Sanctification is not a thing to be picked up at a certain stage of our experience, and forever after possessed, but it is a life to be lived day by day, and hour by hour.

We may for a moment turn aside from a path, but the path is not obliterated by our wandering, and can be instantly regained. And in this life and walk of faith, there may be momentary failures that, although very sad and greatly to be deplored, need not, if rightly met, disturb the attitude of the soul as to entire consecration and perfect trust, nor interrupt, for more than a passing moment, its happy communion with its Lord.

The great point is an instant return to God. Our sin is no reason for ceasing to trust, but only an unanswerable argument why we must trust more fully than ever. From whatever cause we have been betrayed into failure, it is very certain that there is no remedy to be found in discouragement. As well might a child who is learning to walk, lie down in despair when he has fallen, and refuse to take another step, as a believer, who is seeking to learn how to live and walk by faith, give up in despair because of having fallen into sin. The only way in both cases is to get right up and try again.

When the children of Israel had met with that disastrous defeat, soon after their entrance into the [Promised Land], before the little city of Ai, they were all so utterly discouraged that we read: "Wherefore the hearts of the people melted, and became as water. And Joshua rent his clothes, and fell to the earth upon his face before the ark of the Lord until the eventide, he and the elders of Israel, and put dust upon their heads.

"And Joshua said, Alas, O Lord GOD, wherefore hast thou at all brought this people over Jordan, to deliver us into the hand of the Amorites, to destroy us? would to God we had been content, and dwelt on the other side of Jordan! O Lord, what shall I say, when Israel turneth their backs before their enemies! For the Canaanites and all the inhabitants of the land shall hear of it, and shall environ us round, and cut off our name from the earth: and what wilt thou do unto thy great name?" (Joshua 7:7-9, KJV).

What a wail of despair this was! And how exactly it is repeated by many a child of God in the present day, whose heart, because of a defeat, melts and becomes as water, and who cries out, "Would to God we had been content and dwelt on the other side of Jordan!" and predicts for itself further failures and even utter discomfiture before its enemies. No doubt Joshua thought then, as we are apt to think now, that discouragement and despair were the only proper and safe condition after such a failure. But God thought otherwise. "And the Lord said unto Joshua, Get thee up; wherefore liest thou upon thy face?" The proper thing to do, was not to abandon themselves thus to utter discouragement, humble as it might look, but at once to face the evil and get rid of it, and afresh and immediately to "sanctify themselves."

■　　■　　■

"Up, sanctify the people," is always God's command. "Lie down and be discouraged," is always our temptation. Our feeling is that it is presumptuous, and even almost impertinent, to go at once to the Lord, after having sinned against Him. It seems as if we ought to suffer the consequences of our sin first for a little while, and endure the accusings of our conscience; and we can hardly believe that the Lord *can* be willing at once to receive us back into loving fellowship with himself.

A little girl once expressed this feeling to me, with a child's outspoken candor. She had asked whether the Lord Jesus always forgave us for our sins as soon as we asked Him, and I had said, "Yes, of course he does." "Just as soon?" she repeated doubtingly. "Yes," I replied, "the very minute we ask, He forgives us." "Well," she said deliberately. "I cannot believe that. I should think He would make us feel sorry for two or three days first. And then I should think he would make us ask Him a great many times, and in a very pretty way, too, not just in common talk. And I believe that *is* the way He does, and you need not try to make me think He forgives me right at once, no matter what the Bible says."

She only *said* what most Christians *think,* and what is worse, what most Christians act on, making their discouragement and their very remorse separate them infinitely further off from God than their sin would have done. Yet is totally contrary to the way we like our children to act toward us, and I wonder how we ever could have conceived such an idea of God. How a mother grieves when a naughty child goes off alone in despairing remorse, and doubts her willingness to forgive; and how, on the other hand, her whole heart goes out in welcoming love to the repentant little one who runs to her at once and begs her forgiveness! Surely our God felt this yearning love when He said to us, "Return, ye backsliding children, and I will heal your backslidings."

— *The Christian's Secret to a Happy Life,* 1870

# Forget the Salt

*Restlessness and discontent
are the necessities of progress.*

—THOMAS EDISON

I've always thought Lot's wife received a severe, over-the-top judgment when God zapped her into a pillar of salt. After living in a town for years, who wouldn't sneak a nostalgic, backward glimpse while leaving? But evidently God wanted to teach a generation (and us) about the necessity and obedience of forsaking evil and propelling into the future, without longing for or regretting the past.

Forget what's behind. Keep your eyes on the goal. Hope for what's ahead. These messages penetrate the Bible from Genesis to Revelation, forming the rallying cries waved on God's compassionate banners as we march into infinity. In the Bible heaven-marked people didn't grow roots; they traversed from one location to another, from one blessing to a greater grace, if they followed sacred instructions—and despite their previous failings. Abraham pulled up tent stakes in the desert more than once, the Israelites hiked to the Promised Land, Esther *the foreigner* was crowned queen, and Paul embarked on several missionary journeys.

God might not call us to relocate physically, but the principle of forward movement still applies as we forsake sin and pursue his purpose. Pushing ahead, either internally or externally, also depends on courage. Be strong and courageous, God told Joshua before leading the Israelites into the Promised Land (Joshua 1:6). Fear not, the angel reassured Mary when announcing her mission to deliver and raise the Messiah (Luke 1:30, KJV). Don't be afraid, the Lord instructed while telling John to record the book of Revelation (Revelation 1:17). Think of the consequences if just one of these people had caved in to fear and refused the Lord's call. Consider what might happen if we don't forsake sin and persevere in the midst of difficulty. We could miss out on blessing thousands; we might lose the honor of ministering to just one. Either role, or any amount of influence in between, represents a worthy mission if it's issued from God's hand.

Learning from difficulty and catapulting into God's horizon also requires a certain restlessness. Not the discontent of lusting after the world and its happiness, but the desire for fresh, enlarged territory approved by the Lord himself. Jabez, an honorable man but a minor character in the Old Testament, cried to God, "Oh, that you would bless me and enlarge my territory! Let your hand be with me, and keep me from harm so that I will be free from pain" (1 Chronicles 4:10). God granted his request.

There's much preaching these days that we can echo this prayer, and I agree, if we're striving for holiness as Jabez was. It's always more spiritually profitable to uproot and risk traveling behind Jehovah's dense cloud than to stand salty but inert in the sun.

---

*But in keeping with his promise we are looking forward*
*to a new heaven and a new earth, the home*
*of righteousness. So then, dear friends, since you are*
*looking forward to this, make every effort to be found*
*spotless, blameless and at peace with him.*

—2 PETER 3:13-14

# With My God I Can

## *A Prayer for the Persevering*

You, O LORD, keep my lamp burning;
my God turns my darkness into light.
With your help I can advance against a troop;
with my God I can scale a wall....

It is God who arms me with strength
and makes my way perfect.
He makes my feet like the feet of a deer;
he enables me to stand on the heights....
You give me your shield of victory,
and your right hand sustains me;
you stoop down to make me great.

Therefore I will praise you among the nations, O LORD;
I will sing praises to your name.

—PSALM 18:28-29,32-33,35,49

# PART SEVEN

# Foolish for God

Time passes, needs press in, the rope nears breakpoint, but God asks us to wait. We're to wait for his timing, for his answers, for his guidance, for his work in our lives. Waiting leads us to obedience, not only for the time at hand, but for the future. He asks, "Will you follow me? Will you be foolish in the world's eyes for my sake?" Brokenness teaches us to say yes.

We think of obedience as harsh and excruciating, but it's actually practical, keeping us safe from Satan's harm and fortifying our inner life. It woos and rewards us. When we obey, we participate in God's work in us, but also his work in the world.

# Always Waiting

*Andrew Murray*

Therefore, turn thou to thy God: keep mercy and judgement, and wait on thy God continually" (Hosea 12:6, KJV).

Continuity is one of the essential elements of life. Interrupt it for a single hour in a person, and it is lost, he is dead. Continuity, unbroken and ceaseless, also is essential to a healthy Christian life. God wants me to be—and God waits to make me, every moment—what He expects of me and what is pleasing in His sight.

If waiting on God be the essence of true religion, the maintenance of the spirit of entire dependence must be continuous. The call of God, "Wait on your God continually," must be accepted and obeyed. There are many times of special waiting, but the disposition and habit of the soul must be there uninterruptedly.

This waiting continually is indeed a necessity. To those content with a feeble Christian life, it appears a luxury. But all who pray, "Lord! Make me as holy as a pardoned sinner can be made! Keep me as near to You as it is possible for me to be! Fill me as full of Your love as You are willing to do!" feel it is obtainable. They feel there can be no unbroken fellowship with God, no full abiding in Christ, no maintaining of victory over sin and readiness for service, without waiting continually on the Lord.

The waiting continually is a possibility. Many think that with the duties of life it is out of the question. They cannot always be thinking of it; even when they wish to, they forget.

They do not understand that it is a matter of the heart, and that what fills the heart occupies it, even when the thoughts are otherwise engaged. A father's heart may be filled continuously with intense love and longing for a sick wife or child at a distance, even though pressing business requires all his thoughts. When the heart has learned how powerless it is to keep itself or bring forth any good, when it has learned how surely and truly God will keep it, when it has accepted God's promise to do the impossible, it learns to rest in God. In the midst of occupations and temptations it can wait continually.

This waiting is a promise. God's commands are enablings: gospel precepts are all promises, revelations of what God will do for us.

■    ■    ■

When you first begin to wait on God, it is with frequent intermission and frequent failure. But do believe God is watching over you in love and secretly strengthening you in it. There are times when the waiting appears to be just losing time, but it is not so. Waiting, even in darkness, is unconscious advance, because it is God who is working in you—God who calls you to wait on Him, sees your feeble efforts, and works in you.

Your spiritual life is not your own work; as little as you began it, you can continue it. It is God's Spirit who has begun the work in you of waiting upon God. He will enable you to wait continually. Waiting continually will be met and rewarded by God Himself working continually.

Would that you and I might learn one lesson: God must work continually. He does work continually, but the experience of it is hindered by unbelief. But He who by His Spirit teaches you to wait continually will bring you to experience how His work is never-ceasing. In the love and life and work of God there can be no break, no interruption.

Do not limit God in this. Do fix your thoughts on what may be expected. Do fix your eyes upon this one truth: In His very nature, God, as the only Giver of life, cannot do otherwise than to work in His child every moment.

Do not look only at one side: "If I wait continually, God will work continually." No, look at the other side. Place God first and say, "God works continually; every moment I may wait upon Him continually."

Take time until the vision of your God working continually, without one moment's intermission, fills your being. Your waiting continually will then come of itself. Full of trust and joy the holy habit of the soul will be, "On thee do I wait all the day" (Psalm 25:5, KJV). The Holy Spirit will keep you ever waiting.

—*Waiting on God*, 1992 edition

# A Few Good Things

*It's a good thing.*

—MARTHA STEWART

Before I moved out of the house and stacked my belongings in a storage unit, a friend offered this practical advice: "When you move into Mary's place, take along some items that you love. Keep them in your bedroom so you see them every day. They'll be reminders of who you are and where you came from." In other words, she advised me to select a few good things to keep my identity intact and bring me pleasure.

I took her seriously. While packing I carefully added small items to my Few Good Things box. They included a hand-painted pitcher crafted in France; an antique vase once owned by my great aunt; a replica of a turn-of-the century glass biscuit container I received from a friend; a framed photo of my young parents in which they looked particularly handsome; a blue-and-white saucer and tea cup with a lid, part of a set my sister Barb mailed to me; some of my favorite or unread books; and several other framed photographs. I also decided that my original paintings would hang in that bedroom, too, even if they stacked one above the other European style, or somewhere else in the house so they wouldn't disintegrate or be stolen from storage.

The strategy worked. On days I feel bereft of privacy and property, I cradle my few good things and examine the paintings. *This is who I once was,* I think, *and this is who I can be again.* This cheers me.

A couple of other friends who passed through similar paring-down times also offered advice. One said, "Create a routine for yourself." The other insisted, "Do some activities that you love, even if you really can't afford them. You can't afford *not* to, or you'll lose yourself." I accomplish these directives by regularly visiting Starbucks for a latté or Frappucino before invading the office, and occasionally by eating lunch with a girl-friend or attending movies and cultural events.

One month I attended an art exhibit at a major museum—something I used to do regularly when I traveled but now I can't afford—and my soul plumped up. While my niece Melissa and I strolled through the Henri Matisse collection visiting Denver, I tried not to act giddy. I felt like I'd rediscovered old friends, but we only possessed a few hours to soak in everything about one another, everything we'd said and done in those lost years. That night when I returned home, a friend commented, "I wish you could go to an art exhibit every week. I haven't seen you so happy in ages."

During lean or difficult times, it's easy to submerge our authentic selves and what we love. So we need to deliberately nurture ourselves and do what rushes joy through our creative veins. Even though God may be rearranging our habits, character, and circumstances, he still "richly provides us with everything for our enjoyment" (1 Timothy 6:17). Not every day needs to be grim. We can grab moments of delight that refresh and sustain us. We can do what we love without feeling guilty. It's necessary for our well-being and survival, even if it's something cost-free like walking in the park or playing that old guitar.

Trust me, there will be plenty of times to feel sad. So taste joy whenever possible. Treasure a few good things.

---

*Praise the LORD, O my soul, and forget not all his benefits…who satisfies your desires with good things so that your youth is renewed like the eagle's.*

—PSALM 103:2,5

# Small Obediences

*Obedience is rooted in love, not fear;*
*It is activated by affection, not by force.*
*Keeping the commands, for Christians,*
*is not dull rule-keeping but passionate love-making.*

—EUGENE PETERSON

It's probably obvious by now that I was a sensitive child who worried about most everything that matters to kids: whether my friends liked me, if my sister would ever stop heckling me, and especially if I'd fit in and succeed at school. So it was no surprise that the night before a class exam I'd be awake past bedtime, fretting.

One incident in particular protrudes in my mind. Not because the impending threat of another test loomed so large it seared my memory, but because of how my mother managed me and my woes.

I was in the fifth grade, the year children "back then" tackled multiplication tables. With my mom as coach, I'd spent the evening before the test reciting tables over and over, until she finally declared, "No more! You have to go to bed." The next morning she launched me to school with a kiss and a prayer, and I trudged toward the dreaded place that demanded that I, a budding creative and intuitive type, learn how to manipulate numbers.

Despite my preparation and Mom's prayers, the day disintegrated. Most students flunked the test. My teacher, exasperated, made us review the multiplication tables again that afternoon, number by excruciating number. Then she announced, "We're having another test at the end of the school day. And you can't go home until you pass it!" Not a good tactic on my teacher's part, but what else could a bunch of defenseless and stressed-out kids do? We gritted and sweated through the test, rattled by our teacher's disgust.

After I finished I waited in line at Mrs. Sharmin's desk so she could correct my answers on the spot. Would I pass and gain freedom? As I inched closer to her grim face and red correcting pencil, it felt doubtful. So I did the unthinkable. When I stepped close enough, I peeked at her answer sheet, noted the math problems I'd answered incorrectly, and sidled back to my desk to change them. I cheated.

The subterfuge ensured my release, but it awakened a nagging conscience. That night, plagued with remorse and awash in tears, I told Mother what I'd done. Mom gathered me in her arms and explained that she understood my fears, but my decision had been wrong. I needed to ask God to forgive me, and also Mrs. Sharmin.

God I could deal with, but my teacher?

Yes, my teacher.

The next morning, alone but bolstered by my mom's emotional support, I arrived early to school and blurted the wrongdoing to a surprised teacher. But instead of scolding her wayward student, Mrs. Sharmin, startled by the honesty, smashed me to her bosom in a bear hug. She forgave me with soothing words and without punishment. I remember that embrace so vividly I can still smell her awful perfume.

■   ■   ■

When Mom sent me back to school, worried about my fate, she taught me a lesson about honesty that I've never forgotten. In the scheme of life, my infraction probably seemed small to many people, but my mother realized that "little" sins lead to large ones, and small obediences can avert big trouble. From that day through graduate school, I never cheated on a test again.

As we pass through difficult times we often think about the big picture, wondering if we'll recover, anticipating what we'll do next, or waiting for "the other shoe to drop." But per usual God thinks differently than we do. He asks us to focus on the small, daily obediences. These seemingly minor decisions affect how we manage hardship, when our wounds will heal, and who we'll be when the crisis passes. Jesus said, "Whoever can be trusted with very little can also be trusted with much," (Luke 16:10). He referred to the need for honesty, but the principle applies to obedience, too. If we obey God in the small decisions, we'll choose correctly in the big moments. Obeying in heartache sets a pattern for right living when circumstances approach normal again. (If there is such a state as "normal"!)

I wish I could master this wisdom once and for all. Instead, even in my forties I still learn by getting into trouble, needing God to rescue me, then realizing how I might have avoided a fiasco. I should have paid attention to the small moments. I could have obeyed.

I've gathered from pain and hindsight that God doesn't ask us to obey—to follow his biblical directives—so he can hem us in unreasonably and ensure our misery. Rather, he wants us to obey so we'll circumvent the agony and consequences of sin, both for ourselves and others. Viewed from this perspective, obedience is a gift from a loving Father who desires that we live as peacefully as possible on earth.

In turn, we obey out of love and gratitude to God, realizing he keeps our protection and best interests in mind. We love him because he first loved us (1 John 4:19). We obey him during our struggles because "he learned obedience from what he suffered" (Hebrews 5:8) and looked to the joy set before him (12:2). We feel that joy, too, when we follow him.

---

*If you obey my commands, you will remain in my love,*
*just as I have obeyed my Father's commands*
*and remain in his love.*

—JOHN 15:10

# Unreasonable Faith

*I must tell you I take terrible risks.*
*Because my playing is very clear,*
*when I make a mistake you hear it.*
*Never be afraid to dare.*

—VLADIMIR HOROWITZ

During my last years of working for religious organizations, I neglected church attendance with the excuse that I needed a day off from "so many Christians who want so much from me." Overwork and faith had grown synonymous, and I gulped for spiritual breathing room. Even after exiting a Christian publishing house, I avoided religious gatherings for the sake of healing.

Then Joan moved in with me for a few months. My new friend avidly searched for a church for herself and frowned on my Sunday morning mattress time. She also repeatedly mentioned a small congregation she'd visited on occasion, praising the spontaneous worship and teaching sermons. I resisted Joan's unsubtle hints until after she moved out, and then in an attempt to relieve my guilt about church avoidance, I attended a service on my own terms: alone and in a back row. For me, church translated to risk, a place that could bruise me even more.

That initiated months of sitting in services and crying as the Holy Spirit peeled off layers of crusty protective coverings. Eventually I admitted to myself that I needed spiritual healing and personal change. Working as an author of Christian books hadn't exempted me from sin's damage wreaked by others and myself. As I unraveled, two areas of obedience crystallized for me.

First, if I was to handle my finances according to Scripture, I needed to begin tithing again—something I hadn't done for years. Every week before the offering, the associate pastor briefly reminded us that we needed to give to God. My income was dwindling monthly, and it seemed absurd to give ten percent to the church, but I also couldn't afford not to tithe, either. I didn't want to further complicate my financial plight with disobedience, if that was the case. So out of desperation more than anything, I started writing checks to the church when I received payments from clients. Sometimes I mailed the tithe in immediately, rather than waiting until Sunday to drop it into an offering basket, because I feared changing my mind about giving that week. It hurt to relinquish the cash, and there wasn't an immediate return on my investment. A year later I wondered if I'd been duped, but I kept giving with what felt like irrational faith.

Second, I needed the inner healing that forgiveness produced. Again at Joan's suggestion I began meeting with a woman who specialized in helping wounded Christians recover. Over several months we met sometimes weekly, sometimes intermittently, to comb through my life and forgive the people and circumstances that'd hurt me. Aside from one evening when I received a gentle vision, most of the sessions felt rote and unemotional. I'd create a list for a session and with the counselor as witness I'd pray through it, pardoning each person for specific offenses and asking God to forgive me for bitter judgments against him or her. We prayed through a list that spanned infancy to adulthood—through family members, friendships, boyfriends, church members and pastors, work relationships, book editors and publishers, and anybody else the Holy Spirit spotlighted. Again, no kickback materialized for my efforts, and I pushed onward, wondering if I'd confessed for nothing.

These parallel tracks of doubtful obedience coincided with the mandate to move out of my house, so again, it didn't feel as if God had blessed anything. When I piled into Mary's home, I had no money, debts to pay, and zero prospects for new work. After a day or two of fretting, I decided on a last-ditch attempt for funds. I hadn't received royalty statements from one of my book compilations, and I called the publisher to ask if there'd been a mistake. I left a message on voice mail, relieved that I didn't have to embarrass myself "in person," playing the starving artist. The next day an apologetic author relations manager called me and said yes, they'd overlooked paying me. She wanted to send a check to me via express mail. I asked her, "What's the amount you'll be sending?" When she replied, I paused in shock, then asked her to repeat it again. It was the largest check I'd ever received as a writer. Enough to pay sizeable business bills, keep up with current taxes, and not worry about finances for a while.

A few months earlier a speaker at church claimed when she obeyed God and forgave someone, it released something in the heavens that manifested in circumstantial changes. I believe that happened to me, though I doubted and fussed as I complied with the truth. As I trudged in obedience, tithing, and forgiving, God released the blessing of book sales. Financially, he gave back five times more than I'd begrudgingly given to him. (But I probably wouldn't believe this story, unless it happened to me.)

Interestingly, if I'd received the royalty check on schedule, I'd have moved into a home by myself. So I can only conclude that God wasn't finished with me yet; he had more to teach me while scaling down and rooming with another person. Later, I also realized I still couldn't have afforded living by myself anyway. The royalty check didn't produce a lucrative business, but it provided for acute invoices and income at the time. God supplied what I needed in his peculiar timing, then introduced his next lessons.

■　　■　　■

Be careful. Be realistic. Be conservative. These are common messages— and oftentimes the church's warnings—presumably to ensure our personal and financial security. But Jesus taught an unreasonable faith that grasped at the unseen, sold everything to follow him, and slaughtered a person's desires, even obliterated a life, to save a soul and enter God's kingdom. Western Christianity has migrated so far from this sacrificial concept that I think cramming into someone else's house is monumental martyrdom. I consider my minimal expectations and those of my friends (homes, clothes, vacations, investments, furnishings, etc., etc.) and it needles me. Where is our faith, our willingness to risk everything for the Cross? Most days mine's swept under the bedroom throw rug, between the cat hair and the carpet. I admire a Mother Teresa or a Brother Andrew, but am I willing to live like one?

Despite our misgivings God urges us to faithfully exercise our faith, instead of relying on our own devices or the culture's schemes. No matter how you slice it, faith isn't reasonable. It's a leap into what feels like nothingness, the undefinable space of God's promises, with the hope that Someone will catch us. Nonbelievers call faith blind, but the Bible says it's "the substance of things hoped for, the evidence of things not seen" (Hebrews 11:1, KJV). Sometimes the only "evidence" we can dig up are the claims of Scripture and the stirring in our hearts. But that's more than many biblical people possessed—before the full revelation of God's Word—and the New Testament applauds them for their faith (see Hebrews 11). Could it be that the information glut and our ingrained materialism mar our ability to perceive what's spiritually apparent, to vault into faith? I wonder.

I also wonder—despite all I've lost so far—when I'll wholly comprehend what it means to live by faith. I'm scared to hope it's soon; I'm also scared not to.

---

*Now the just shall live by faith:*
*but if any man draw back,*
*my soul shall have no pleasure in him.*

—HEBREWS 10:38, KJV

# The Harder Thing

*Elisabeth Elliot*

How long will you go limping between two different opinions?'" Elijah
asked the people of Israel. "'If the LORD is God, follow him; but if Baal,
then follow him'" (1 Kings 18:21, RSV). The people had been thrown
into confusion by Ahab the king, and Elijah was sent to straighten them
out. It was a question as to which god was the true one. Clearly, it had to
be one or the other. Elijah the prophet and truth-teller was not really welcome, for he would clarify the issues and force the people to a choice.

But such clarification and pressure is exactly what is needed where
there is confusion, and it is exactly what the Word of God does. It strips
away whatever is irrelevant and dispenses with the side issues, "piercing
to the division of soul and spirit, of joints and marrow, and discerning
the thoughts and intentions of the heart. And before him no creature is
hidden, but all are open and laid bare to the eyes of him with whom we
have to do" (Hebrews 4:12-13, RSV).

Most of us avoid crises when we can. It is far more comfortable to
sit in the back row than to stand up and be counted. It is less demanding to fade into the crowd, stay in the shade, move at our accustomed
pace. To take up the cross and follow, to walk in the light, to climb the
steep ascent of heaven are not options that have a strong popular appeal.

But we are speaking of those who actually want to do the will of
God. What we are concerned with now is the business of choice when
both alternatives seem equally moral. Choose the harder of the two
ways. If you have eliminated all other possibilities and there still seem to

be two that might please God, choose the more difficult one. "The way is hard, that leads to life," (Matthew 7:14, RSV) Jesus said, so it is likely that he is asking us to will against our will.

But what if he isn't asking that? The more sincerely we seek the will of God, the more fearful we will be that we may miss it. If it made little difference to us, obviously we would not worry very much about it, so there ought to be a measure of reassurance for us in the very fact of our fear. Jesus is in the boat with us, no matter how wild the storm is, and he is at peace. He commands us not to be afraid.

The supreme example outside that of our Lord himself, of a man willing against his own will, in obedience to God, is Abraham. He was asked to sacrifice Isaac, his only son—and this, in the face of all God's promises about descendents. Abraham was to tie the boy down on top of a pile of kindling on an altar. This he did (with what anguish we can only imagine), and only then, when with the knife poised he had triumphantly passed the hardest test of faith, did God show him that his son's death was not finally required (Genesis 22).

David was willing to undertake a staggering project, the building of a temple for God. God did not allow him to build it but was pleased with him for wanting to. "You did well that it was in your heart," (1 Kings 8:18, RSV) God told him.

When Paul, Silas, and Timothy were traveling together as missionaries in Asia Minor, "they attempted to go into Bithynia, but the Spirit of Jesus did not allow them" (Acts 16:7, RSV). We could wish Luke had told us exactly how the Spirit of Jesus stopped them, but it is enough for us to know that the men who were bent on obedience to God had made, in the integrity of their hearts (we may believe), a wrong decision and that God reversed it.

"And your ears shall hear a word behind you, saying, 'This is the way, walk in it,' when you turn to the right or when you turn to the left" (Isaiah 30:21, RSV).

— *God's Guidance*, 1997

# Keep Me Steadfast

*A Prayer for Those Wanting to Obey*

Blessed are they whose ways are blameless,
who walk according to the law of the LORD.
Blessed are they who keep his statutes
and seek him with all their heart.
They do nothing wrong;
they walk in his ways.
You have laid down precepts
that are to be fully obeyed.
Oh, that my ways were steadfast
in obeying your decrees!
Then I would not be put to shame
when I consider all your commands.
I will praise you with an upright heart
as I learn your righteous laws.
I will obey your decrees;
do not utterly forsake me.

—PSALM 119:1-8

# The Protective Hedge

*Take care of me, because it is for you*
*that I am suffering.*
*Lord, protect your servants:*
*stay with them to the end,*
*and then they will be able*
*to glorify your name for all eternity.*

—EUPLUS

My friends know that whenever I write a book, the spiritual warfare heats up. I've been accosted so regularly I can almost predict the types of attacks the devil plans for me. During the months of producing a manuscript, usually a relationship problem erupts; the computer fritzes and needs repair; my health declines or my body develops unusual quirks; one of my cats creates a crisis by getting ill, dying, or running away; my cash flow dries up; something in the house or car malfunctions; and confusion or depression descend on me. The predictability would be laughable if it weren't so frustrating, so destructive to my deadlines. Besides, now that I've admitted this, the pattern will probably change.

Through the years I've learned to wage spiritual warfare that's redemptive, the kind that banishes Satan and his minions and restores my body and peace of mind. But now I'm adding in preventive precautions. I'm asking God to build a protective hedge so the attacks won't debilitate me at all. These offensive walls assemble through prayer, claiming scriptures, worshiping God, playing praise tapes, and generally staying spiritually alert. I don't know why it's taken so long to think of this. The last few weeks have been so calm I barely know how to work. I've grown accustomed to writing midst a battle.

A few days ago I received this e-mail from one of my prayer team members: *Judy, a word of encouragement. As I was praying for you the other day, the Lord gave me a vision of you at a desk, writing. You were encircled by demons and evil spirits trying to get at you. But the good news is that they couldn't reach you because there were angels with large wings in a circle facing you, standing gold wing to gold wing, holding them back. You were head down writing and did not even notice the peril you were in. I will continue to pray for focus, protection, and a keen ear. We will talk soon. Love, Kathie.*

I wrote back to Kathie and explained that now I knew what to ask for when I prayed, and I would imagine this comforting picture as I worked. Whether we're in difficulty, emerging from hardship, or just moving through our days, it's a protection we can request from God. "For he will command his angels concerning you to guard you in all your ways; they will lift you up in their hands, so that you will not strike your foot against a stone. You will tread upon the lion and the cobra; you will trample the great lion and the serpent. 'Because he loves me,' says the LORD, 'I will rescue him; I will protect him, for he acknowledges my name'" (Psalm 91:11-14).

Sometimes God even warns us to pray for protection. I recently met a woman from Littleton, Colorado, whose sons were in the Columbine High School library when two armed students entered and started shooting. The morning of the tragedy, Susan felt strongly impressed that her teenagers were in danger, so she interceded for their safety. Later she learned that a gun had also been pointed at her daughter, but none of her children were hurt.

That's not to say Susan was "more spiritual" than the Christian parents of students who were killed or maimed or traumatized. Nor does he care more about her family than the others. It remains a mystery why certain children escaped and others didn't. But this does graphically illustrate that, when we feel a nudge to ask for protection, it's always good to err on the side of caution and pray until the burden lifts.

Regarding spiritual warfare, we don't know what will happen next. But God does, and we can call on him.

---

*May the LORD answer you when you are in distress;*
*may the name of the God of Jacob protect you.*

—PSALM 20:1

# The Mark of the Christian

## *Francis Schaeffer*

When everything is going well and [Christians] are all standing around in a nice little circle, there is not much to be seen by the world. But when we come to the place where there is a real difference and we exhibit uncompromised principles but at the same time observable love, then there is something that the world can see, something they can use to judge that these really are Christians, and that Jesus was indeed sent by the Father.

Let me give [a] beautiful example of such observable love. [It] happened among the Brethren groups in Germany immediately after [World War II].

In order to control the church, Hitler commanded the union of all religious groups in Germany, drawing them together by law. The Brethren divided over this issue. Half accepted Hitler's dictum and half refused. The ones who submitted, of course, had a much easier time, but gradually in this organizational oneness with the liberal groups their own doctrinal sharpness and spiritual life withered. On the other hand, the group that stayed out remained spiritually virile, but there was hardly a family in which someone did not die in a German concentration camp.

Now can you imagine the emotional tension? The war is over, and these Christian brothers face each other again. They had the same doctrine and they worked together for more than a generation. Now what is going to happen? One man remembers that his father died in a concentration camp and knows that these people over here remained safe. But people on the other side have deep personal feelings as well.

Then gradually these brothers came to know that this situation just would not do. A time was appointed when the elders of the two groups could meet together in a certain quiet place. I asked the man who told me this, "What did you do?" And he said, "Well, I'll tell you what we did. We came together, and we set aside several days in which each man would search his own heart."

Here was the real difference; the emotions were deeply, deeply stirred. "My father has gone to the concentration camp; my mother was dragged away." These things are not just little pebbles on the beach, they reach into the deep wellsprings of human emotions. But these people understood the command of Christ at this place, and for several days every man did nothing except search his own heart concerning his failures and the commands of Christ. Then they met together.

I asked the man, "What happened then?"

And he said, "We were just one."

To my mind, this is exactly what Jesus speaks about. The Father has sent the Son!

Love—and the unity it attests to—is the mark Christ gave Christians to wear before the world. Only with this mark may the world know that Christians are indeed Christians and that Jesus was sent by the Father.

*—The Mark of the Christian, 1970*

# PART EIGHT

# Broken and Blessed

What are the blessings of brokenness? They may be different than we think, focusing on character rather than materialism. These blessings signify the fruit of God's work in our lives, the qualities that resemble him, rather than our mark on the world. Though God may bless us in many ways, we're to walk humbly with him.

But even when the journey "smoothes out," he asks us to continue living with a spirit of brokenness. Will we remember the lessons imbued in God's hand? Hopefully, time in the shadow will affect how we live in the light.

# The Blessings of Brokenness

*In the depth of winter,*
*I finally learned that within me*
*there lay an invincible summer.*
—ALBERT CAMUS

What good is all this suffering, anyway? It makes a person miserable!"
I agree, but over the years I've realized that sometimes misery budges me toward spiritual growth and personal change. Though we're still in process, we can look back and identify alterations that hardship sliced and razored into our lives, if we allow God to realign us through the pain. At the time, it may not feel like we're progressing spiritually. In fact, it seems like we're rapidly regressing, but eventually treasured spiritual qualities can emerge from our dark night of the soul.

Ponder these transformations that I've noticed in people who've suffered. I call them the blessings of brokenness.

- Difficulty draws us closer to God in his Word.
- We more readily recognize our transgressions and repent of them.
- Pinpointing our sin, it's easier to forgive those who've hurt us.
- The prayer life deepens and we depend on it for strength.
- Sharing in the sufferings of Christ conforms us to his image.
- Pride diminishes and we walk more humbly before God and others.
- Suffering softens the personality, mellowing difficult character traits.
- Passing through hardship develops mercy and compassion.

- Pain compels us toward breaking the bondages we're trapped in.
- We loosen our grip on trying to control our lives and others.
- Our spiritual eyes better perceive biblical truths and the unseen world.
- Kingdom values grow more urgent than worldly pursuits.
- We sharpen our desire and ability to wage spiritual warfare.
- We exercise and increase our faith in God's acts and character.
- Hope and endurance rise up in ways we never thought possible.
- We understand this world is not our home, and we long for heaven.

Essentially, we discover that what dwells inside people holds more value than what appears on the outside, and we search for and respect others who've developed internal fortitudes, stamped on their souls through difficulty. Hopefully, we are never again the prideful frights we were before. But most important, we cherish the blessings of brokenness because they're the fruit of God's righteousness exuding from us.

---

*It was good for me to be afflicted*
*so that I might learn your decrees.*

—PSALM 119:71

# What Does
# the Lord Require?

*An able and humble man*
*is a jewel worth a kingdom.*

—WILLIAM PENN

When I taught high school journalism, on the first day of a semester-long class I'd extol the virtues of taking the course, the topics we'd cover, the projects we'd complete. I attempted to build enthusiasm in students who genuinely wanted to acquire the knowledge, and to weed out those who thought an elective course would produce easy credits toward graduation.

No matter what I said, though, it didn't seem to matter. Students looked glazed over until one of them asked the inevitable question, "What are the requirements to get a good grade?" By this the teenager meant earning the top-ranked A, and suddenly everybody perked up. With the exception of a few students I immediately adored, the collective body language explained, "We don't care about learning to write, we just want a good report card." After I described the requirements, some groans floated toward me, and the next day I received a computer printout of names who'd dropped the class.

At least I collected fewer tests and assignments to correct.

We tend to carry over this just-give-me-the-requirements approach to God, and I'm no exception. During trying times we ask, "What does God want? I wish he'd reveal what I'm to learn so I can stop struggling!" We think if he'd just hand us a list of requirements, a spiritual lesson could be mastered quickly and then discarded, except for the solid A marked on heaven's permanent records.

Eventually we discover that God's lessons can be lifelong and that sometimes he reveals his intentions, but sometimes he does not. He simply asks us to persevere, cooperating with what we know to do and cultivating humility. That's called faith. Later we might understand the Lord's lesson, or maybe just how we grew and changed through the difficulty. There's no precise answer about whether God will unfold his plan, on earth or in heaven, but we can trust that his motivations are good and his lessons prove beneficial (Psalm 34:8; Nahum 1:7). That's called maturity.

Maturing in faith also means caring about God's pleasure after the trouble passes. Relieved by the problem's resolution—or our distance from the difficulty—we forget to ask, "Lord, what do you require now?" Presuming his answer, my list would look like this: (1) Don't get into trouble anymore. (2) Be perfect. (3) Do all the correct religious rituals. But centuries ago God presented his three-point list through the prophet Micah. He said, "And what does the LORD require of you? [1] To act justly and [2] to love mercy and [3] to walk humbly with your God" (Micah 6:8).

God's requirements emerge so drastically different from mine, at first glance I barely comprehend them. Roughly translated, God asks that we offer the same justice and mercy to others that he lavished on us and that we kneel humbly before him. From his lifelong lessons we're to flow in lifetime love.

---

*Sacrifice and offering you did not desire,*
*but my ears you have pierced;*
*burnt offerings and sin offerings*
*you did not require.*
—PSALM 40:6

# The Parable
# of the Lost Sheep

## Fiction by Melissa Munro

What's it like to be a sheep? To lie on your back, feet flailing in the air, kicking, struggling to get up? To hear his voice calling my name? I hear it and cry out, a soft, desperate bleating. He keeps calling. I try to stand up.

At first I'm wrestling on my own, not wanting his help. *I wandered off. I got stuck. I ended up on my back, unable to right myself. I will get back on my feet by myself.* But the more I try to extract myself, the deeper I sink. For a moment I'd been comfortable and unafraid, then I remembered that sheep can die this way. Now I'm frantic. I have to get up, get out of this. But I can't move. Will I die here in humiliation?

Then I hear his voice again, a distant tone. I stop struggling and strain to listen. A faint sound caresses my quivering ear. I hear my name…it must be my imagination. How could he be looking for me? I know I'm not supposed to stray off, but when this started I was only a little lost. I might have found my way home. But now I'm helplessly stuck and maybe hurt. I'm no use to him as a sheep. I'm not a very good sheep anyway. I don't follow him well. I wander off.

His voice draws nearer to my helplessness. I'm afraid to respond, afraid for him to find me, afraid of what he'll do. Yet he's the only one who can rescue me, so I cry out. I bleat again and again. I cry stronger each time I hear my name. Then I hear his voice change. He's heard my call. Uncertain that he's glad to find me, I bleat again. His voice sounds closer and lighter, as if a load just lifted off his shoulders.

Soon he's hovering over me and I can't believe the joy on his face! He pulls me up and cradles me in his arms for a moment, checking for injuries. His hands feel gentle, warm. It's been a chilly wait with fearful shivers robbing any warmth from the quickly setting sun. He sets me down and I panic again. *Is he leaving me here? It'd be what I deserve.*

"Be at peace little lamb," he says. Then he kneels down and swings me onto his shoulders. They're bony but full of muscle from carrying other sheep, and it's not the most comfortable place in the world. He has a death-grip on my feet and I wonder if I'll ever walk again. But here I am safe. Nothing can harm me. I don't struggle across the rough terrain, stumble into hills, or scratch myself on thistles.

Still, I don't really like this position. It means the world will see I've been lost. They'll know the Shepherd had to search for and carry me. I don't like to show my failures to them. At the same time, I'm proud that the Shepherd loves me this much! He loves me so much that he carries me. Even though I've failed, even though others might leave me for dead, he carries me home like a trophy! I'm the saved one!

The path looks familiar yet I wonder where we're going. This isn't the way to the sheepfold. Then I spot the roofs of the village. People appear in doorways, some calling out to the Shepherd, wondering why he carries me. He calls back, telling them he's found his one lost sheep.

"Where are your other sheep?" they ask him. "Why did you save that one?"

"He's a fool a to leave the others for this one," some mutter. "What if the wolves attack while he's away? He could lose everything he owns!"

And yet a few stop and stare. They see the love in the shepherd's eyes, feel it radiate from him as he gently soothes me. Then I understand that when I'm weak, he'll be strong. When I'm at my worst, he lifts me up and shows his love to the world.

"What do you think? If a man owns a hundred sheep, and one of them wanders away, will he not leave the ninety-nine on the hills and go to look for the one that wandered off? And if he finds it, I tell you the truth, he is happier about that one sheep than about the ninety-nine that did not wander off" (Matthew 18:12-13).

—Journal Entry, 1998

# The "I Did It" Syndrome

*O Lord, forgive what I have been,*
*sanctify what I am,*
*and order what I shall be.*

—THOMAS WILSON

For reasons I've forgotten, I stayed away from the office that morning, and after a late breakfast I switched on the television for background noise while tackling some housework. The familiar voice of a talk show host boomed from the tube. *What's he got people riled up about now?* I wondered and stepped into the bathroom, cleanser and scrub brush in hand. I turned a faucet handle, and over the splashing and scouring, the television blared an answer.

That day's entertainment began with a lineup of guests espousing the joys of weight loss. Then to spice up their lean cuisine stories—and the audience's response—the host pitted them against a double-chinned lady who insisted that fat is beautiful. I abandoned a half-clean sink to view the woman. With four ex-fatties against her, I knew she'd wind up emotionally carved to the bone, and for the next half-hour I dipped in and out of the bathroom, watching the screen more than the porcelain.

My sympathies sided with the fat lady. At one point her husband, thin as a Popsicle stick, emerged from the audience to deliver his homily, "Why I Love Her Just the Way She Is." I admired his devotion. But the overweight wife couldn't bask in his love for long. Immediately another female guest countered with a hard-edged sermon about "What's Terribly Wrong with Obese People." I resented her arrogance.

Just when I'd nominated the slimmed-down lady as Most Opinionated Person of the Year, she concluded, "I was right to lose the weight, and I give all the credit to the Lord!" Scattered whoops erupted from the audience, as if to confirm that haughtiness is acceptable if it evokes God's name.

It's wonderful to conquer a sin or be released from suffering. It's the heart of the gospel to embrace and enjoy redemption, to celebrate God's goodness to his children individually, especially when we're the recipients. But when we've been rescued from trouble, we also land in a spiritual danger zone. If we've finally "gotten the victory," we usually want others to get it too, but if we're not sensitive, our tactics can harm more than help. We might even accomplish the opposite of our intentions. For example, after we've conquered a sin or situation, it's tempting to condemn it in others. Or we could expect them to "find release" exactly the way we did, and push for compliance. We might as well ask, "I did it, why can't you?" Or the more guilt-provoking question, "The Lord did it for me, why isn't he doing it for you?" That's what the misplaced zeal communicates. Consequently, we discourage rather than inspire those who still struggle and need hope. We minister from pride rather than compassion.

We've also forgotten who's in charge of the redemptive process. The Lord—not us—delivers the desperate, and he works uniquely and creatively in each person's life. After salvation through grace, our ongoing redemption may not look like someone else's. (Actually, everyone's coming-to-salvation story differs, so why do we expect similarity in how people grow spiritually?) To insist on squeezing others into our mold could hinder the Holy Spirit's movement in them and block their progress. Instead, we're to humbly live our deliverance before others, remembering the apostle Peter's words: "All of you, clothe yourselves with humility toward one another, because, 'God opposes the proud but gives grace to the humble'" (1 Peter 5:5).

Scripture also says that pride appears just before a fall (Proverbs

16:18). Ever known anyone who preens about a weight loss, then gains it back? Or someone who's unusually vocal about kicking an addiction, then succumbs to it again? It's as if an invisible rope tied around the neck pulls a bragger back into the pit. In the early days of my career, I attended a weeknight Bible study with other professionals. One night I sat through the study like a predator waiting to pounce. When we reached the "share and prayer" time, I burst with the news: "Praise God! For a whole month now, I've had a quiet time with God every single day. That's a real victory for me!" I blabbed with superiority for a while and noticed that some faces dropped lower and lower as I talked. *They must feel guilty because they're not seeking the Lord the way I am,* I thought. *I'm determined to never repeat my sporadic devotions of the past.* And I kept my resolve. Within a few months I wasn't having devotions at all.

Humility seems like the obvious choice once we've messed up and needed God's forgiveness ourselves. But it's astonishing how quickly the soul practices amnesia if it's no longer in pain; we can drift from God as our source and fall prey to the "I did it" syndrome. However, a good way to circumvent this downfall is to remember the golden rule and ask, "How would I like to have been treated while still struggling? How can I share my victories so they communicate hope, not condemnation?" It's remarkable how quickly clarity returns once we think about that.

---

*So in everything, do to others*
*what you would have them do to you.*

—MATTHEW 7:12

# My Portion Forever

## *A Prayer for the Heaven Bound*

[God,] I am always with you;
you hold me by my right hand.
You guide me with your counsel,
and afterward you will take me into glory.
Whom have I in heaven but you?
And earth has nothing I desire besides you.
My flesh and my heart may fail,
but God is the strength of my heart
and my portion forever.

Those who are far from you will perish;
you destroy all who are unfaithful to you.
But as for me, it is good to be near God.
I have made the Sovereign LORD my refuge;
I will tell of all your deeds.

PSALM 73:23-28

# In the Now

*The vocation of every man and woman*
*is to serve other people.*

—LEO TOLSTOY

I do not think grandly when I wake up in the morning. Usually my mind focuses on two routine duties, both motivated by necessity. The first is: *I have to go to the bathroom.* The second: *I have to let out the cats.* Until I navigate these urgencies, my mind stays in neutral, so I felt startled one morning to wake up to an unexpected agenda. As soon as I opened my eyes, the plan for a specialized writers' retreat presented itself, sitting on my brain, as if it'd been waiting for me to stir.

*How strange,* I thought. *Where did this come from?* I hadn't been musing about the idea the night before or, for that matter, aspiring to start new projects. I had a book to write and that felt like enough. Still groggy with sleep, I rolled over, only to be greeted with specific instructions. *Start up a weekend retreat for women,* said the voice in my head. *But not just any women. It must be for women who want to minister through the written word. The ones who'd be serious about it. Hand select the participants from women you already know and pour your knowledge into them. Teach them about the writing life. Prepare them for influence.*

I rolled back again, pondering the possibility. *This might be God,* I thought. *I wouldn't have thought of this, especially not the first thing in the morning.* Besides, the idea made sense. In the past few years at out-of-town retreats and conferences, I'd met women who'd confided they felt called to write, but didn't know how to begin. My spirit resonated with their desire to publish—I thought God may be calling them to minister through writing—but given the circumstances, I could only offer them a few encouraging insights. But bringing them to my town to teach them? That might work.

By the time I fired up the coffeemaker, the idea captivated me, and I breathed a hesitant prayer. *Okay, God, I'll make a list and write letters,* I told him, dropping a little toe into the waters of faith. *But I don't have the money to invest in this and these women are very busy leading their own ministries and raising families. It seems impossible they'd all have the same weekend open. If this is really from you, they'll be available and say yes.*

Several days later I devised a rough budget for the weekend, including food, lodging, transportation, and materials, and gave God my financial criteria, as if he didn't already know my needs. *Lord, if this is from you,* I said, repeating uncertainty, *then I'll need at least ten women who can pay enough to cover the expenses.*

*Plan it for the first weekend in October,* came the reply.

A few weeks later, after the idea burrowed deeper into my heart, I sent an invitation letter to fifteen women. Would they be interested? Or would they laugh? I'd soon find out. However, instead of dictating a date, I asked the women to vote for which of four weekends in September and October would best fit for their schedule. In the next month ten women replied with a yes, and when I tallied their preferences, they all had the same time slot open; the first weekend in October. I knew I had to quit second-guessing God, follow instructions, and march.

■　　■　　■

Over the next few months, the participants increased to twelve, and the retreat fell into place in a way I'd never experienced before. (I'm accustomed to wrestling project details to the ground, but for this event the particulars embraced me.) Women volunteered to help facilitate the weekend, two of my publishers contributed money, men and women covenanted to pray for individual participants and their needs—the list continues. During my research for a book project, a name emerged for the gathering: the Vision Group, based on the Habakkuk verse, "Write the vision, and make it plain upon tables, that he may run that readeth it" (2:2, KJV). I'd heard that when God initiates a project it flows in ways we'd never manage on our own. The retreat was becoming living proof. The Lord knew what he was doing; I only had to follow along and watch him perform.

A few weeks before the retreat, as I considered what I'd teach the group about writing, another unexpected instruction walked across my mind. *Be willing to set aside your agenda and follow mine.* Now this felt more challenging. I'd taught many writing classes, and, good or bad, my teaching style crammed in as much information as possible, complete with handouts to take home. *Set aside my notes and wing it?* Already I was concerned about not having enough time for all the "necessary" information. *What would we do?*

Based on God's performance so far, I decided to trust him with this directive, too, though I'd never taught this way before. Curiously, I wasn't the only one "in the dark" about the weekend. Several participants had sent notes that admitted, *I don't know why I'm coming to this. I just know God told me to come.* At least we'd all be clueless together.

True to his word, God intruded on the first teaching session. As I talked about the characteristics of writers, I asked, "As a child, alone in your room, did you write?" If the answer is yes, this frequently indicates a writer has been born. A few minutes later two women interrupted me, one after the other, to say they'd just flashed back to a long-forgotten childhood incident. In each case the woman wrote something meaningful to herself, but an insensitive family member ridiculed her writing. Both felt that, without their realizing it, the ridicule materialized into a fear that blocked them as adults from writing. Soon after this revelation, during break time a few participants prayed for these women, asking God to release them from fear.

*Amazing,* I thought. *God, what else will you do this weekend?* It didn't take long to find out. That session set the pattern, and for three days I rearranged my lectures to make room for ministry. Collectively, we confronted other fears about writing, prayed for physical ailments that hinder the creative process, counseled and interceded for women with emotional wounds, sought God for direction in each woman's life, listened to his prophetic words to us, and drank in his vision and renewal. Revealing the specifics would break confidences, and I don't know everything God accomplished when women formed friendships, talked in their hotel rooms at night, strolled around the premises, or huddled in small prayer or discussion groups. I don't need to know. Watching God work was plenty![13]

However, I understand a couple of other things. First, when God calls us to do something, we might miss wonderful surprises if we refuse. This fall marks our fifth year for the group, and it seems every gathering improves upon the last. Each year we lose a few members, add some new ones, and a handful of women have attended every retreat. They're publishing articles and books, fulfilling their dreams, and deepening friendships. At each retreat I'm overwhelmed by God's good idea and the privilege of knowing these women and speaking into their lives. Last year I expanded the program to four retreats in various locations, and the honorariums I receive for leading and teaching fill in some financial gaps between writing projects. God not only fulfills these women's desires, but He also provides for me. I learn as much from them as they do from me, and to top it off, a few give me stylish and thoughtful gifts each year.

But the second thing I've learned is the truly astonishing one. God didn't wait until my troubled times had subsided, or until I'd finally worked through His list of personal changes for Judy, to ask me to serve. He called me in the middle of hardships and doubts and setbacks, with my obvious character and spiritual and professional flaws, to flesh out his plan. I didn't need to be perfect, at the top of my profession, or even positive that the retreats—or, for that matter, my life—would be successful. I only had to cooperate with him.

I believed God ultimately uses our difficulties to comfort and assist others, but, given my circumstances, I relegated those responsibilities and rewards to sometime "out there" in the future when life settled. In my opinion, I shouldered enough and wasn't searching for more. But God asks us to serve in the now, and he carves out the time and desire to minister. We don't need to be in sterling shape to extend our hands and pray for someone, to share our dilapidations with a hurting person, to teach from what we've learned by our mistakes so far. If our stories point the struggler to God, then we've advanced his kingdom.

Serving from the center of life's challenges keeps our words credible, the applications fresh, and our dependence on God thorough. It also rewards us with a profound and indescribable joy. Who could ask for anything more?

---

*Now is the time of God's favor,*
*now is the day of salvation.*

—2 CORINTHIANS 6:2

# Living in the Light

## *John of the Cross*

God takes time to prepare the soul that He wants to lead onward, with patience and gentleness. His Majesty allows us years to accustom ourselves to the spiritual life in general, and that is because of the limitless forbearance and kindness that flow from His vast love.

Yes, as we first begin our deeper walk in the Spirit, He will indeed lead us through intense trials of faith and emptiness, which feel like traveling through a spiritual wilderness. As you come out of such a time, you will feel as if you have been purged. You will find yourself in a place of great peace. It is as if you have made a breakthrough and escaped from a hard imprisonment into an open land of running springs.

The soul feels as if a new well has been opened up within it. Up from this new stream of God's Spirit, there flows a sense of greater freedom from the circumstances of life, which used to control and trouble the soul. The soul no longer has to work itself up with "spiritual thoughts," in order to find this place of inner rest. For the waters of this stream continually flow without any help or effort from us at all. They are always flowing up from within to soothe the soul whenever it becomes fretful, distracted, or anxious.

In another way of speaking, it is as if the soul has climbed to a higher place, a place of serene rest. And from this new height, it can look down and examine both the earthly things that would attack its peace and its own inner weaknesses, which make it subject to attack.

So the soul experiences far more freedom and happiness than it did in the beginning, before it learned how to rise above the dark night of its natural senses and earthbound ways of thinking.

As I have said, God allows us time to become stronger and more proficient in our ability to walk this way, in the Spirit.

Others may notice striking changes in you—a new kind of light and purity coming from inside.

And this is only a beginning. It is like the hopeful radiance of a bride who is preparing for union with her Lover. To think—this is the same Light that shines upon those who have already passed into the untellable joy of heaven. And it shines upon those of us here below, who are still being made ready.

*—Dark Night of the Soul, 1500s*

# What Matters Most

*God gives his servants a taste in this life,*
*yet the harvest and the vintage are to come,*
*when they that suffer with Christ Jesus*
*shall reign with him,*
*and they that have sown in tears*
*shall reap the never-ending harvest*
*of inconceivable joys.*

—ROGER WILLIAMS

Last week my father's sister hovered near death, her vital organs shutting down from diabetic complications. Through the family grapevine I heard that the doctor considered my aunt clinically dead for about ninety seconds, but she rallied and stabilized. Later she told a hospital worker, "I went to heaven, but I didn't see anyone I knew there, so I came back." I hope my aunt was spoofing us, but if not, that's a sobering observation, a family wake-up call to drop the Christians on their knees.

I've felt the fragile curtain between life and death flutter several times in recent years, but the most agonizing was almost losing my mother. Dehydrated and depressed and drenched in physical pain from several undiagnosed or uncontrolled symptoms, she called me on the phone, her voice barely recognizable, asking me to drive to Phoenix immediately. She feared dying soon, and it frightened me, too.

One terrible trip later, I watched Mom sleep unsoundly after surgery, with tubes and other contraptions invading her body. She looked weathered, not like the mother who'd always appeared a decade younger than her age, but I recognized the knobby, deeply veined hands and stroked them. In those lonely moments what mattered most focused sharply, like never before. It wasn't my work, which pressed in heavily that month; or my income, which would decline because of the unexpected travel; or my dream home, which might not ever exist; or pleasing anybody in the world, which felt increasingly impossible anyway. It was our hope and security in God. My mother was prepared to meet him, but selfishly, I wasn't willing to release her into heaven.

Due to my sister's perseverance with the medical practitioners and the Lord's mercy, Mom survived and celebrated her eightieth birthday. But daily I'm reminded that her life hangs precariously between this breath and a last gasp, though I pray the finale still resides years away. But as Mama contemplates heaven, which she frequently talks about, what would she say matters most? As I wonder about the end of my days, what will I regret? What will I be grateful for? These questions help me unearth meaning in my current dilemmas, centering on eternal values rather than obsessing about what will wither and evaporate in God's purifying presence.

For me, it's the providential purpose of pain to reduce my focus to what truly matters, letting the insignificant debris turn ashen and whisk into oblivion. An old adage says, "Only one life on earth will pass; only what's done for Christ will last." Growing up, I heard those words so many times, it nauseated me. Now I want to breathe them.

---

*For no one can lay any foundation other than the one*
*already laid, which is Jesus Christ. If any man builds*
*on this foundation using gold, silver, costly stones, wood,*
*hay or straw, his work will be shown for what it is, because*
*the Day will bring it to light. It will be revealed with fire,*
*and the fire will test the quality of each man's work.*

—1 CORINTHIANS 3:11-13

# Psalm 20

May the LORD answer you when you are in distress;
may the name of the God of Jacob protect you.
May he send you help from the sanctuary
and grant you support from Zion.
May he remember all your sacrifices
and accept your burnt offerings. *Selah*
May he give you the desire of your heart
and make all your plans succeed.
We will shout for joy when you are victorious
and will lift up our banners in the name of our God.
May the LORD grant all your requests.

Now I know that the LORD saves his anointed;
he answers him from his holy heaven
with the saving power of his right hand.
Some trust in chariots and some in horses,
but we trust in the name of the LORD our God.
They are brought to their knees and fall,
but we rise up and stand firm.

O LORD.... Answer us when we call!

# Notes

1. Unknown Christian, The Cloud of Unknowing, ed. William Johnson (New York: Image Books, 1973), 53.
2. Faith Forsythe in *Tid-Bits,* quoted by Frank S. Mead, *The Encyclopedia of Religious Quotations* (Old Tappan, N.J.: Revell, 1965), 1.
3. Padraic Colum, introduction to *The Complete Grimm's Fairy Tales* (New York: Pantheon, 1944), xiv.
4. Anna Quindlen, *One True Thing* (New York: Random House, 1994), 14.
5. Quindlen, *One True Thing,* 157-8.
6. Barbara Kingsolver, *The Poisonwood Bible* (New York: HarperCollins, 1998), 13-9.
7. Kingsolver, *The Poisonwood Bible,* 515.
8. Kathleen Norris, *The Psalms* (New York: Riverhead, 1997), viii.
9. Eugene H. Peterson, *Praying the Psalms* (Grand Rapids/New York: Zondervan/HarperCollins, 1993).
10. John Ortberg, *Love Beyond Reason* (Grand Rapids: Zondervan, 1998).
11. Frederick Buechner, *Wishful Thinking: A Seeker's ABC* (San Francisco: HarperSanFrancisco, 1993), 24.
12. Saint John of the Cross, *Dark Night of the Soul* (New York: Image/Doubleday, 1990).
13. The opening story first appeared in another book by Judith Couchman, *His Gentle Voice* (Sisters, Oreg.: Multnomah, 1997). Used by permission of Multnomah Publishers.

# Credits

# Contributing Authors

M. Craig Barnes is an author and pastor of the National Presbyterian Church in Washington, D.C.

E. M. Bounds spent the last seventeen years of his life reading, writing, and praying. He wrote many classic works about prayer, which have stayed in print for almost a century.

Jamie Buckingham, an ordained minister, published many articles and over forty books. He also served as a contributing editor to magazines and was spiritual overseer of his church.

Frederick Buechner has been honored by the American Academy and Institute of Arts and Letters and nominated for a Pulitzer Prize for his novel *Godric.* He is also the author of many other fiction and nonfiction books.

Oswald Chambers moved from evangelist to college teacher to spiritual shepherd for troops at war in Egypt. After Oswald's early death, his wife compiled his sermons posthumously, leading to *My Utmost for His Highest,* a classic devotional.

John of the Cross was a spiritual mystic of the sixteenth century who, through opposition and danger, helped many find love and freedom in Christ.

Brent Curtis worked as a counselor and, with coauthor John Eldredge, wrote *The Sacred Romance.* They also presented the Sacred Romance lecture series, using music and movies to illustrate their teachings.

Elisabeth Elliot is the best-selling author of many books, including *Shadow of the Almighty.* She is a popular seminar leader and hosts the radio program *Gateway to Joy.*

Debra Evans lives in Austin, Texas, and is an educator, speaker, and author of numerous articles and more than a dozen books.

HANNAH HURNARD served as a missionary to Israel and wrote eight books, including the perennial best seller, *Hinds' Feet on High Places.*

SUE MONK KIDD, a longtime editor at *Guideposts,* is the author of many articles and several books.

BRENNAN MANNING, author of various books, spends much of his time traveling, directing spiritual retreats, and writing.

F. B. MEYER was an English minister who pursued social concerns and wrote many devotional and expository books.

MELISSA MUNRO, who works in the editorial department of NavPress, has published her first article.

ANDREW MURRAY served many years as a pastor, writer, and missionary in South Africa. He's best known for his books on prayer and abiding in Christ.

KATHLEEN NORRIS is an award-winning author and poet who wrote about her life as a Benedictine oblate in the best-selling book, *The Cloister Walk.*

HENRI NOUWEN was a Catholic priest who taught at several theological institutes and universities. He wrote many books and later in life ministered to the disabled.

FRANCIS SCHAEFFER founded the L'Abri Fellowship in Switzerland, published many books, and was a noted speaker throughout the world.

HANNAH WHITALL SMITH was a Quaker teacher in the nineteenth century. Her most popular book, *The Christian's Secret of a Happy Life,* has stayed in print over one hundred years.

PAUL TOURNIER, M.D., lived and worked in Switzerland as a doctor, counselor, and author of many books.

WALTER WANGERIN JR. is an award-winning author who holds the Jochum Chair at Valparaiso University, where he works as writer-in-residence.

# About the Author

Judith Couchman, the owner of Judith & Company, devotes her work time to writing, speaking, and sponsoring seminars. She's the award-winning author or editor of many books, Bible studies, compilations, and Bible projects. In addition to writing, Judith leads the Write the Vision retreats and seminars for writers, and the Designing a Woman's Life seminars to help women find their purpose in life.

Judith was the founding editor-in-chief of *Clarity* magazine and has served in several editorial and management positions in publishing and organizational communications. She has received national recognition for her work in education, public relations, and publishing, and holds a master's degree in journalism and a bachelor's degree in education.

Some of Judith's books include *A Garden's Promise, Designing a Woman's Life, One Holy Passion, Shaping a Woman's Soul,* and *The Woman Behind the Mirror.* She lives in Colorado.

To learn more about Judith's books, seminars, and retreats, visit her Web site at http://www.judithcouchman.com.

# OTHER WORKS
## BY JUDITH COUCHMAN

### BOOKS

*His Gentle Voice*

*A Garden's Promise*

*The Woman Behind the Mirror*

*Shaping a Woman's Soul*

*Designing a Woman's Life*

*Lord, Please Help Me to Change*

*Lord, Have You Forgotten Me?*

### BIBLE STUDIES

*Deborah: Daring to Be Different for God*

*Esther: Becoming a Woman God Can Use*

*Hannah: Entrusting Your Dreams to God*

*Mary: The Joy of Choosing Obedience*

*Celebrating Friendship*

*Designing a Woman's Life Bible Study*

*Why Is Her Life Better Than Mine?*

*If I'm So Good, Why Don't I Act That Way?*

*Getting a Grip on Guilt*